STARTING A FLOWER AND GIFT SHOP

by

Dr. Millicent Gray Lownes-Jackson

Edited by

Dr. Leah Grubbs

A BUSINESS OF YOUR OWN ®
BUSINESS PUBLICATIONS AND SERVICES FOR WOMEN
www.ABusinessOfYourOwn.com

TM

CONGRATULATIONS!!!

By merely opening this publication you have taken the first step toward self-fulfilment, financial independence and taking control of your life. You obviously have an interest in small business ownership and desire to take the informative approach to starting your own business. Effective application of the information presented in this publication will enable you to fulfill your dream of business ownership and financial success. This publication will take you step-by-step through the process of business formulation. At the end of your reading, you will have produced a business plan for your dream and will have identified the specific steps you need to take for implementing your business to be competitive.

A BUSINESS OF YOUR OWN is here to help you pull together the intricate components necessary to make your small business a success. We offer various support services as well as numerous business publications to assist you in pursuit of your entrepreneurial dreams.

We invite you to take the entrepreneurial challenge and wish you much success!

www.ABusinessOfYourOwn.com
Mailing address: P.O.B. 210662, Nashville, Tennessee, 37221-0662 (615) 646-3708

OUR SYMBOL   **A ROSE OF PURPLE**

A BUSINESS OF YOUR OWN will help you till the soil and prepare fertile ground for the growth and development of a strong and successful business venture. It will take time. It will take shrewd business savvy. It will take planning and re-planning and it will take an honest assessment of yourself.

Rose gardens don't just happen overnight. A rose, purple in color, demands very special attention and a great amount of time for development and much nurturing. But, there are few flowers more special that a beautiful, unique rose. The cultivation of a beautiful purple rose is representative of the development of your successful business venture.

The purple rose is distinctive and different. It represents newness, freshness, femininity, and taking the challenge to be different.

Women have intrinsic characteristics that, like a purple rose, can be cultivated. These characteristics can be channeled into a viable avenue of financial independence. But, a woman does not have to lose her uniqueness of being a woman.

A rose of purple, just like a business, requires much time, attention, dedication, knowledge, and nurturing. **A BUSINESS OF YOUR OWN** is here to help you in developing your unique rose.

Our goals are to help cultivate your abilities, assist you in channeling your attributes successfully into a business of your own, encourage you to be the best you can be, provide information to help make you successful in the business world and at the same time encourage you to maintain your identity and femininity.

A Business of Your Own
BUSINESS PUBLICATIONS & SERVICES FOR
WOMEN
P.O.B. 210662
Nashville, Tennessee 37221-0662
www.ABusinessOfYourOwn.Com
E-mail: Success@womaninbiz.com

INFORMATION ABOUT THIS PUBLICATION

The entrepreneurial informational publications of A BUSINESS OF YOUR OWN reflect an enormous amount of in-depth research and the expertise of many noted professionals. In addition to keeping abreast of industry and environmental changes along with new business management techniques and concepts, our staff compiles and presents this information in a readily applicable, easy-to-understand format. Obtaining detailed industry information as presented in our publications would have taken your complete business venture concentration for many, many months. In addition, by purchasing our publications you will avoid the costs that would have been incurred in consulting many professionals and the stress encountered in determining business development procedures.

All information contained in this publication will need to be applied to your particular operating environment as each environment is unique and exciting. We, therefore, cannot accept responsibility for your success; but we truly believe that the information and the step-by-step approach utilized in this publication will assist you in making more intelligent decisions about the initiation and development of your business.

Even though all companies, resources, and organizations mentioned in this book are believed to be reputable, A BUSINESS OF YOUR OWN cannot accept responsibility for the activities of these parties, nor is A BUSINESS OF YOUR OWN attempting to promote their business efforts.

Congratulations on taking the first step to business success by obtaining the necessary knowledge to realize your dreams.

"To be successful in entrepreneurship, you must first begin with the spirit. With your spirituality in order, you can conquer all things."

M.G.L.J.

TABLE OF CONTENTS

CHAPTER I

Introduction

"Whenever times get tough, just pause

and count all of your many blessings."

M.G.L.J.

INTRODUCTION

The quest for business ownership is still very much a part of the American dream, and the entrepreneurial spirit is alive and strong for women. Offering for many, a feeling of personal worth, wealth, prestige, and a way of controlling one's own time and destiny, female-owned businesses represent the fastest growing business sector of the economy. Recent private research conducted by the Center for Women's Business Research reports that, as of 2002, there were an estimated 10.1 million majority-owned, privately held 50 percent or more women-owned firms in the United States, employing 18.2 million people and generating $2.32 trillion in sales. Of this 10.1 million, 6.2 million are majority (51%) or more women-owned, and 3.9 million are 50 percent women-owned firms. As of 2002, there were an estimated 1.2 million firms owned by a woman or women of color-amounting to 1 in 5 women-owned firms (20%) in the U.S. Overall, the number of minority women-owned firms increased by 32 percent between 1997 and 2002--four times faster than all U.S. firms and over twice the rate of all women-owned firms. Between 1997 and 2002, the Center estimates that the number of privately held 50 percent or more women-owned firms increased by 11 percent nationwide, nearly twice the rate of all firms; employment increased by 18 percent, and sales grew by 32 percent. [1]

Census Department data uses different definitions for women-owned businesses, requiring that the business be 51 percent owned by a woman before it is classified as woman owned. Thus, Census data reports a fewer number of women-owned businesses, but the bottom line is that women-owned businesses are playing a vital role in the U.S. economy. Women-owned businesses are growing more rapidly than the overall economy and are major contributors to the nation's economic health and competitiveness. Many of these women-owned firms are considered to be micro-enterprises, small businesses with fewer than five employees. Generally, these businesses are characterized by a net worth of less than $25,000 and a credit need of less than $15,000. Many of the business owners are women who are underemployed or have low incomes.

National research recently conducted by this writer utilizing survey research methodology provides additional insight into practical entrepreneurial knowledge. Surveys were disseminated via a national business publication as well as a local community newspaper. The survey was designed to ascertain pressing concerns, problems, and stressors experienced by female business owners. A summarization of the findings indicates the following areas of concern as identified by female micro-enterprise owners: organizational ability, selling skills, finding and keeping good employees, managing stress, inequities due to race or sex, inability to obtain government and corporate accounts, inability to break the "ole boy" network, inability to obtain sufficient capital, inability to effectively and efficiently manage operating expenses, feeling isolated, managing time, and the challenge of accepting all responsibility. The issues and concerns raised by this survey population of 200 female micro-enterprise owners reflect the views of those who have taken the entrepreneurial plunge and have provided a sound academic and practical base for compiling the relevant and valuable information contained in this publication.

FLORAL INDUSTRY OVERVIEW

If you enjoy working with flowers and plants, if you enjoy working in an environment filled with fragrant, natural beauty, if you enjoy supervisory tasks, if you are creative and can design store and display windows and can effectively and efficiently perform various business responsibilities, then owning a flower shop may be your opportunity for freedom in using your talents, expressing your artistic ability, and earning a substantial income without having to conform to limitations imposed by someone else.

The market for flowers can lead to a blooming business if you have the creativity and business savvy to rise above the competition. According to the Society of American Florists, "Floriculture item sales at retail were estimated to be $19 billion in 2003 with average annual florist shop sales being $250,191."[2] Flowers are used to celebrate any and every occasion; and the previous upper income purchaser of flowers has moved over, allowing those with less income to significantly alter the flower market. The categories of flower purchasers range from those who buy flowers and plants regularly for enjoyment to those who buy only for specific reasons and special occasions. The buyers are mostly women from age 24 and up, with the majority falling between 24 and 45.

The flower industry, however, still depends heavily on the yearly cycle of flower gift giving--in spring, Easter, Mother's Day, and graduations; in summer, weddings; and in fall and winter, Halloween, Thanksgiving, and Christmas. Birthdays rank second in non-calendar occasion buying of floral items, with fresh cut flowers being selected the majority of the time for birthday gifts which are typically bought for a friend, mother, or wife. According to the

American Floral Endowment, birthday gifts of flowers are particularly purchased when the person is hard to buy for or the purchaser just couldn't think of anything else to buy.[3]

In addition to the seasonal impact on sales, the industry has also been impacted by consumers' desire for convenience. On-line shopping, telephone networks such as FTD, street vendors, and supermarket/convenience store sales of flowers have impacted the sales of the small flower shop owner.

Gifts are a natural complement to flower offerings and afford the flower shop owner an opportunity to distinguish herself from competitive mass marketers. The gift retailing industry depends heavily on the yearly cycle of gift giving just mentioned for flower shops; and since flower buyers are often buying flowers as a gift, offering additional gift options simply expands your revenue possibilities. Gift items could consist of brass items, novelties, collectibles, candles, wedding party gifts, stationery, imprinted napkins, unique sympathy tokens, gift baskets, special teas and tea pots, balloons, cards, stuffed animals, elegant vases, crafts made by local artisans, dish gardens in elaborate ceramic planters, and any items that complement a gift of flowers. The selection of gifts is only limited to your imagination, the nature of your shop, and what you think your market would desire.

THE FLOWER SHOP OWNER

The mere love of flowers and being creative are not enough to be successful in operating a flower shop. The owner of a flower shop should have some formal education in the floral arena. Experience in the industry is also highly desirable. Many colleges and universities offer courses and degrees in floriculture. There are also floral design schools throughout the country that offer short courses in floral design. In addition, the flower shop owner needs a basic knowledge of business and management.

The owner of a flower and gift establishment needs to be a people-oriented person. She should like working with customers and should have the ability to give customers a "warm and fuzzy" feeling when they enter the establishment. The owner must also be able to convey this to other employees who serve customers. The retail store owner must really be in tune with the desires of her customers and must have the ability to purchase what they want. This is often more difficult than it sounds. If ongoing market research is not conducted, the owner will not know what customer needs are. At the same time, all desires cannot be researched; a lot is left up to the "gut" feeling of the flower store owner.

The business owner must, of course, reflect on all of the marketing information presented in this publication and be able, through researching and studying the market, to answer the questions of **who, what, where, when** and **why** of consumer buying habits and choices.

The **who** refers to the customers identified as being in the business owner's target market. The **what** refers to the types of merchandise these potential customers want to buy and, therefore, **what** the flower shop owner should stock. The **where** refers to the trading area from which the business attracts its customers. The **when** refers to the part of the year when the customers make their purchases. The **why** refers to psychological factors which cause customers to buy.

In conjunction with purchasing, and based on target consumer desires, the flower and gift shop owner must also consider where she is trying to position the business in terms of the reputation she is attempting to develop relating to price, value, quality, and assortment.

LOCATION CONSIDERATIONS

Locating in hotels, near hospitals and funeral homes, in shopping centers, and in neighborhood strips are all alternatives for flower shops. When determining a location for your flower shop, focus on the groups of consumers who frequent flower and gift shops. Locating near or in a hospital allows you to capture the market of flowers for the sick. Locating near a funeral home allows you to penetrate the market for funeral arrangements. Hotel shop locations allow you to develop sales for decorating parties, conventions, and banquets held in the hotel.

Flower shops located in shopping centers tend to have a more generalized trade with a primary focus on flower gifts. Neighborhood shops and strip shops also cater to a general market for party needs, weddings, hospitals, and business accounts, as well as funerals.

Older communities tend to have more need for flowers because of the high frequency of sickness and funerals. Younger communities tend to have more of a demand for flowers for entertaining, general beautification, and gift-giving purposes.

Many shops will choose an initial base location for their flower shop and then, in light of the additional markets they desire to penetrate, open small branch locations. For example, a neighborhood shop may open a branch in a large hotel to capture the needs of the hotel. Sometimes the hotel will make favorable compromises to be able to offer flower services as part of their marketing package to conventions, meetings, banquets, and guests.

Even though you will conduct a great amount of your business by phone, it is important to select a location that will continually attract new business. In general, flower shops should try to locate in areas where the average income is sufficient to support the types of floral products they wish to sell. However, there must also be a desire for floral items.

THE FLOWER SHOP AND THE INTERNET

As more and more people have become comfortable buying merchandise on the Internet, more consumers are also turning to the Internet for floral purchases. While your initial thoughts about this probably question the desire of individuals to purchase such perishable items as flowers on the Internet, The American Flower Endowment has conducted research which found that one in every ten dollars spent for floral arrangements was spent online. [4] This research also found that the greater percentage of floral items purchased online tend to be fresh cut arrangements that are purchased for gifts and went further to suggest that online gifts increase with the likelihood of the recipient residing outside the local area of the buyer. Individuals attracted to online floral purchases tend to be younger and more affluent than the typical floral buyer. [5]

The online expansion of the floral industry opens many opportunities for the small business owner who is savvy enough to have a Web site. An attractive, current, and easily navigated Web site can positively impact the bottom line for the small flower and gift shop owner by not only adding another dimension to your channels of distribution, but also by making potential customers aware of your product line offerings and thus attracting them to your establishment. That busy businesswoman who comes into your shop only at Christmas with a list of friends and family members she needs to send floral arrangements to would find the convenience of being able to select items she wants from the comfort of her home most appealing. She could order from the Internet or fax or phone you a list of her desired items and the persons to whom the floral gifts should be sent. The fact that your competition may have a Web site and you don't may cause you to lose her as a customer.

Now, just having a Web site will not turn your computer into a cash register. The Web site must be marketed. The Web site should be included on your business cards, stationery, gift card inserts for floral arrangements, and of course, should be listed with search engines in order to maximize the benefits of having a Web site.

Why advertise on the World Wide Web (www)? The reasons are numerous. In addition to establishing your presence and enhancing your image in the market alongside your competition, the www allows your firm to reach a large mass market of educated consumers. The Web is available 24 hours a day, 7 days a week, year round. The results of Web advertising are immediately measurable interactively, pages are accessed free of charge, there are no costs to customers for obtaining information, and materials can be updated or changed at any time.

Successful marketing on the Web involves a multi-layered, interactive approach that keeps visitors interested. It should make visitors to your home feel involved and make them interested in touring your business. You can also have fill-in forms which allow you to collect data about visitors to your site as well as distribute documents or software by allowing them to download directly to their computers from your Web site. And certainly the inclusion of an e-mail address creates a link from your home page to your office for addressing further reader inquiries.

To connect to the Internet, you must pay for access through network access providers. These providers offer a range of services and applications that can be tailored to your specific needs. There are many different types of Internet providers which include commercial online access services such as America Online. Costs for your Web site will vary.

Ten years ago, a flower business with a Web home page was unique; but now it is basically expected, especially among businesses that wish to be thought of as technologically advanced and recognized for their business savvy. To maximize your use of the numerous technological advances in the area of computer marketing, you should contact a computer consultant who can assess the actual needs for your particular business and design your Web site.

STORE DESIGN

It is important for retail establishments to stay progressive, not only with merchandise and marketing venues, but also in store layout, fixtures, design, atmosphere creation, etc. Periodic visits to merchandise marts and flower shop establishments in large cities can keep the flower retailer full of fresh, innovative and exciting ideas for encouraging sales.

The design of a flower shop is of utmost importance, as it must create an aura that will make individuals want to enter your establishment, browse, and buy. The atmosphere must inspire customers to buy, buy, buy and feel good about buying from you.

The exterior and interior of the facility must be consistent with the image you have established for your firm, just as everything you do must project the same image down to the packaging and the tissue paper used to wrap delicate flowers for customers. Plans for your business must not only examine the need for your product and service but also the functionality and design of the facility that will be used for the business locations. In planning for a flower shop facility, four key areas need to be addressed.

1) exterior design of the building,

2) the sales or display area,

3) the work area and delivery area, and

4) the office.

The Exterior Design

The exterior should identify your business by a readily visible sign using your business logo. If feasible, the exterior should also consist of display windows which contain merchandise that captivate in a quick glance and show your best floral arranging abilities. Color and style are important for exterior design and should incorporate the color motif in your logo. These elements should also be tied into the business image and flavor which you are attempting to project to the public. Since the nature of flower shops relates to beauty, it is particularly important for the exterior of the facility to be attractive.

The Sales Area

Interior appearance, of course, is important for generating sales. Store layout is also crucial. The layout and design of your flower shop and the attractive display of merchandise are all a part of effective selling.

The sales area needs to be planned so that merchandise can be displayed attractively and that an atmosphere be created that entices one to buy. Beautifully created floral arrangements, attractively displayed and appropriately priced, will make selling easier and will increase the amount that customers spend. Try grouping merchandise intended for similar functions and make sure the sales area reflects the image and color scheme you have selected for your business.

The design should allow customers the option of browsing and, at the same time, lead them to purchasing. Develop a traffic pattern in your store. If customers can simply walk into the center of your store, take a quick glance around and easily walk out, your objective of selling has not been accomplished. Some retailers use a flow plan that forces customers to pass all of the merchandise. Some use nooks and crannies to entice customers.

The salesroom design and merchandise mix should also encourage impulse buying. When customers are waiting for arrangements to be made or when they are paying for merchandise, "cute" little gifts of knickknacks should be visible for spontaneous buys. A good location for novelty craft items made by community residents is the area near the cash register. You will look like a good citizen by supporting community constituents; at the same time, you make a little money from the sale. You can also work out reciprocity arrangements with the craftspersons to have your cards or even your floral arrangements in their establishments.

Proper lighting is an important element in a flower and gift shop. Dramatic and appropriately designed lighting helps create an environment conducive to selling. Lighting should be selected to bring out the beauty of floral colors, encourage shopping, and help create the atmosphere you desire. Appropriate lighting for effect must also be determined for your display refrigerator, store display windows, gift display cases, and work area. Professional lighting consultants are available and can help you determine your lighting requirements.

Simple things such as lighting conducive to buying, plush carpet, and the type of store fixtures or display tables on which merchandise is placed, can add the inspiration to buy. Interior design and layout must be supplemented with pleasant salespeople and, perhaps, even complimentary beverages and/or candy to create that "warm and fuzzy" feeling. You will have to decide what is right for you and your environment, taking into consideration the space you have to work with and the image you are trying to project.

The Work Space and Delivery Area

The workroom must be designed with function in mind. It must be well planned to provide ease of operation and safety. If your shop is very small, you may be the only employee; or at times, only one or two employees are in the store. If this is the case, the employees may have to be floral arrangers as well as salespeople. This means that when not waiting on customers, they are working in the workroom. Therefore, the workroom should be designed so that the sales area is visible to enable the employees to know when customers enter the store. Placing a bell or chimes that ring gently and pleasantly when the door is opened may be desirable and may enhance the desired aura as well as alert sales people to an arriving customer. The workroom should also be situated near a separate entrance for receiving incoming merchandise and sending out deliveries.

Safety is important in all businesses. With flower shops, safety precautions are particularly important due to water spillage on floors. Floor covering should be selected that is not slippery when wet. Flower shops often use rubber tile or rubberized carpeting materials.

The Office

A location for keeping records, answering the phones, and maintaining delivery schedules is a must. The office should be pleasant, comfortable, and functional. It does not need to be especially large, as this is space that will not make you money but is essential for keeping your business organized.

SOURCES OF SUPPLY

Florists have various options from which to obtain inventory and supplies. Plant growers and wholesale florists supply flowers and foliage plants; garden supply distributors provide potting soil, plant food, gardening tools, gardening books, flower pots, and miscellaneous supplies. Various supply companies provide macramé hangers, unique planters, and gift items. The owner of a progressive flower and gift shop may also want to attend a gift show at one of the regional merchandise marts to identify unique gift items or planters.

The flower and gift shop owner should make a point of buying from suppliers, also called vendors, who stand behind their merchandise and offer speedy delivery, good prices, credit and quality products.

According to the Society of American Florists, approximately 70 percent of fresh cut flowers sold in the United States are imported, with the majority of cut flowers being imported from Columbia, California being the top flower-growing state in America.[2] You don't have to go to Holland to buy your bulbs. Appropriate suppliers and wholesalers can be identified by examining indexes such as The Thomas Register, as well as your local yellow pages or local business directory. Each supplier, however, will need to be examined individually; and some trial and error will have to occur before you can identify the vendors most in tune with the complete personality and needs of your business.

The buying aspect of a flower business requires knowledge of flowers and experience, along with a keen ability to evaluate customer demands and, at the same time, be progressive with purchasing decisions. Most flower and gift shops buy from diverse suppliers and attempt to vary merchandise offerings frequently. Of course, it is important to identify the suppliers with whom you feel very comfortable concerning product quality, terms of payment, delivery time, and return policies.

It is important that a business not be developed relying totally on one supplier. If the business encounters problems with this one supplier or the supplier is slow in the delivery of purchases, the entrepreneur's operations may be significantly affected. It is best to use several supply sources continuously so as to establish good credit and rapport with these firms. Resultantly, the entrepreneur will get better service once he or she is recognized as a consistent customer.

Gift shops have many supplier options. Gift retailers can buy directly from manufacturers or through manufacturers' representatives, wholesalers, import sources, and/or independent crafts people, just to mention a few. Distributors, importers, manufacturers, and crafts people all display gift items at trade shows which are held periodically throughout the year in different sections of the country. Trade shows are a great way to discover new products, learn new marketing strategies, and obtain updates on trends in the industry.

The merchandise gift marts which follow not only feature trade shows, but are also the home to numerous resident vendors offering unique and brand-name items. Often times brand recognition of gift items on the part of the customer is an important determinant in selecting vendors. It would be wise to contact the major merchandise marts to see when shows are occurring.

MAJOR GIFT MARTS

NEW YORK	New York Merchandise Mart 41 Madison Avenue New York, NY 10010 (212) 686-1203 www.41madison.com
DALLAS	Dallas Market Center 2100 Stemmons Freeway Dallas, TX 75207 (214) 655-6100 or 800-DAL-MKTS www.dallasmarketcenter.com
ATLANTA	Atlanta Merchandise Mart AMC, Inc./AMERICASMART$^®$-ATLANTA 240 Peachtree Street, Suite 2200 Atlanta, GA 30303 (404) 220-3000 www.americasmart.com
CHICAGO	The Merchandise Mart, Chicago Chicago, IL 60654 (800) 677-MART www.merchandisemart.com
LOS ANGELES	The L. A. Mart Los Angeles, CA 90007 1.800.LAMART.4 www.lamart.com
MIAMI	Miami International Merchandise Mart 777 N.W. 72nd Avenue Miami, FL 33126 (305) 261-2900 www.miamimart.net

A word of caution when visiting a merchandise mart to incorporate gift items into your product offerings: Don't get caught up in the excitement of the moment. It is frequently difficult to attend a trade show or visit a merchandise mart and not get excited and buy things you like or things that are "cute" or "pretty" versus what will sell.

When attending a merchandise mart or trade show, be prepared for vendors setting dollar amount or quantity minimums for initial and often subsequent orders. A good initial strategy is to collect information and catalogs from all the vendors in which you have an interest. Study their catalogs, pricing, normal retail mark up, terms of sale, order minimums, and delivery time and make decisions carefully when you have quiet time to think rather than get caught up in the excitement of a trade show and make hasty decisions.

Shows require specific business credentials and show registration. Contact the show sponsors to obtain details and requirements for participation prior to making travel arrangements. And, remember, you need to do your homework before attending a show. Some shows feature cash and carry vendors which means you will have to be prepared to buy on the spot to get show deals. Study the vendors who will be displaying, and study the exhibit hall and/or mart layout.

The retail store owner needs to have merchandise and buying plans to guide in purchasing the right products at trade shows, merchandise marts, or from appropriate vendors. We will discuss these plans later in this publication.

Vendor Terms

Buying terms are very important to cash-flow concerns. Buying terms are often directly related to a good credit rating. A good credit rating will allow you to obtain "NET 30" terms, allowing payment within 30 days after invoice date. This, of course, allows you to use your money for that period rather than allocate cash when the order is placed.

Some suppliers offer terms such as "2/10" or "1/10," meaning that retailers may take a two percent or one percent discount if the bill is paid within 10 days of the invoice date. Many times suppliers will not tell you of these term possibilities, so do not hesitate to ask. You have nothing to lose.

Other terms to ask about are quantity discounts and freight allowances in which the supplier agrees to pay the freight costs. Freight costs can really add up, ultimately passing the extra cost on to the customer. Freight costs raise your price per item which could affect your competitive position in the market.

Suppliers generally have minimum orders, but many will allow you to purchase less than the minimum with an additional cost being incurred by you. In some cases, incurring the additional cost may be feasible.

Establishing Credit with Vendors

Establishing credit with vendors is a tough area. When you are new and approach a supplier about trying to establish credit, the supplier will ask you for credit references from other vendors. But how can you have credit references from other suppliers when you are a new business?

You will need to identify suppliers who are well-known and willing to work with new firms. It may require a lot of research and face-to-face contact with suppliers at a merchandise mart or trade show to identify good suppliers who are willing to work with new firms attempting to establish credit.

Buy from the supplier several times and pay with a check. Be able to present a letter of credit worthiness from your banker. This may have to be a letter regarding your personal accounts if your business account has no track record. The company, of course, is going to wait until your check clears the bank before shipping the merchandise. After this is done with several orders, you will have established credit with them; and then that supplier can be used as a reference for other vendors. Clarify on the front end at what point you will be able to establish credit or at what point they will bill you versus requiring cash. Also clarify when they will serve as a reference to other vendors.

THE MERCHANDISE PLAN

The successful flower and gift shop owner must develop a merchandise plan with all of the previously mentioned factors in mind. The merchandise plan is often a six-month plan, but this can vary depending upon the merchandise and the desires of the retailer.

The first six months (really six and one-half months) include January, February, March, April (spring), May, June, and July (summer). This plan should be finalized the previous August. At that time, you can assess the demands you experienced during the previous six-month period and accurately make predictions for the same period the following year. This allows you to take advantage of end-of-season buys for non-perishable merchandise. (Don't, however, get too bogged down with too many good buys that must be held in inventory for six months, which will tie up money, and could become obsolete or may not be desirable the following year.) The process of utilizing a merchandise plan also allows you to order from suppliers in foreign markets and from vendors that may be slow on delivery but have desirable merchandise at very good prices. The merchandise plan further ensures that you will have the right merchandise when customers want it.

The second six-month period (five and one-half months) includes August, September, October (fall), November, December and January (winter). This plan should be finalized the previous February for the same reasons stated earlier.

When developing a six-month merchandise plan, consider stock requirements, net sales estimates, reductions in the value of your inventory, available money, and seasonal sales requirements. The merchandise plan also relates to the purchase of perishable floral items such as lilies for Easter and poinsettias for Christmas or the winter holiday season.

The merchandise plan should be translated into a buying plan which calls upon the retailer to actually think about and write down all plans for purchasing or buying. The secret to the success of this plan, as well as the selling plan, is for the retailer to actually follow the plan and not just write it down, put it aside and forget it. The buying plan should detail when the retailer should visit the market to see and evaluate new purchase options for the coming season, when commitments should be made for purchasing merchandise and when the first delivery should be received at the store.

THE SELLING PLAN

The selling plan relates directly to the buying plan implemented by the retailer. Once the merchandise has been purchased, plans must be formulated to ensure the sale of the greatest number of items. The selling plan details when items should be promoted through advertising, window displays, and interior decor changes; when the inventory should be peaked to assure adequate merchandise on hand for higher demand periods; when reorders should no longer be placed; when "markdowns" from regular stock should be taken; and when all merchandise in stock should be sold.

Needless to say, the flower and gift store owner needs to stay abreast of trends in the industry, as well as changes in the environment, economy, and consumer demand. Reading trade journals and belonging to appropriate associations is a "must" for retail selling success.

BUYING PLAN WORKSHEET

ITEM	SUPPLIER	ADDRESS, PHONE, E-MAIL	DISCOUNT	MINIMUM ORDER	DELIVERY TIME	FREIGHT/ DELIVERY COSTS *

*Make sure you know who is responsible for paying freight or delivery costs.

33

INVENTORY

Inventory refers to stocks of anything necessary to conduct business. Merchandise stocks in a flower business generally represent a portion of the business's investment but only contribute to profit when they are actually sold. Small businesses cannot absorb the losses incurred from managing inventory poorly. It takes quite a bit of skill to manage inventory effectively. If you have too much inventory which does not sell quickly, significant funds will be tied up and, of course, spoilage will occur. On the other hand, if you have too little inventory, and customer demands and requests cannot be met, you may lose valued and potential repeat customers.

If customers come in requesting merchandise that you should have, but they are not able to obtain from you, they will go somewhere else. Thinking it is a waste of time to frequent your establishment, they probably will not return to your store when they need the same or a similar item again. You can probably recount your own personal experiences of this nature.

With a flower shop, you want to make a conscious attempt not to overstock due to spoilage. Your new stock should be kept separate from your older merchandise, and of course, you want to use the older merchandise prior to the newer flowers.

Suppliers can be of great assistance in determining your inventory requirements as well as display ideas. After relationships are established with floral suppliers, they will probably call you daily or every other day to determine your needs. They can also tell you about special purchase options.

Inventory Guidelines

Consider the following guidelines as you develop your inventory plans.

- Maintain a good assortment of merchandise--but not too much.

- Make sure your merchandise is in accordance with your store image.

- Keep inventory turning over.

- Know what and how much inventory to order.

- Know when to order inventory and what price to pay.

- Make sure items bought for inventory produce a profit.

- Never rely solely on one supplier

Inventory Records

During the first year of operating your flower business, it is very important that you keep good inventory records to enable you to determine the appropriate flowers and amounts to purchase in future years. At first it will be difficult to precisely determine when to order additional merchandise, but this process will become easier as you become more experienced.

Regardless of the size of the inventory carried, retail establishments need to have an inventory record keeping system to manage inventory effectively. Many small retailers with relatively few items in inventory use manual inventory control systems. In addition, many small retailers use card records, inventory tags, and accounting information to compute the data needed to establish their order points and the best order quantities. Of course, there are well-designed computer programs to assist you with all of your inventory, record keeping, and financial data needs. It is recommended that you obtain the services of an unbiased computer specialist (one not trying to promote a particular computer or software system) to provide guidance with these aspects of the business.

Simple, inexpensive measures of inventory control include:

- Visually examining inventory periodically to determine when additional inventory is needed.

- Physically counting a small portion of inventory each day so that each segment of inventory is counted every so many days on a regular basis.

If your business is not computerized, especially consider:

- Using a stub control system which allows the retailer to retain a portion of the price ticket when the item is sold. The retailer then uses the stub to record the items that were sold.

- Using a written-sheet system which enables the retailer to record the item sold (at the cash register) on a sheet of paper.

The inventory control system used, be it simple or sophisticated, will need to include a process for recording merchandise when it arrives with a verification check to make sure it is what was ordered and it is in good condition. Your accountant can also be of great assistance in setting up your inventory control system.

PRICING

Pricing is a difficult area for flower retailers. Each item you carry must pay for the shelf it sits on, and that includes all of the overhead such as electricity, sales personnel, and operating expenses associated with the item. In determining price, therefore, there must be a sufficient **markup** over the price you paid for the item to cover all direct and related costs and to give you a reasonable profit. At the same time, your pricing needs to consider the image you are trying to project and to account for the price at which your competition is selling similar merchandise.

Merchandise which does not sell ties up your money and keeps you from purchasing new items, and old flowers die. Your **markdown** strategy needs to be well planned. Some flower shops have a major sale once or twice a year to clear out silk flower arrangements and gift items. Some owners will mark plants and non-perishable products down a certain percentage after a couple of months, with an additional percentage taken off every two weeks or every month thereafter until they sell. Ultimately, the **markdown** strategy decision rests with the flower shop owner. Certainly for fresh flowers, you need a plan to buy inventory in accordance with what you can quickly use. For flowers close to spoilage, another plan needs to be in place for markdowns or donations to hospitals or extended care facilities.

Flowers generally have at least a 100 percent mark up over your cost. Additional costs are added on when designing and delivery takes place.

FIXTURES AND EQUIPMENT

The actual fixtures and equipment you need, of course, will vary, based on the individual nature of your business, your store design, and your image. Basic fixtures and equipment for flower shops include, but are not limited to, the following:

- Refrigerator for flowers (The refrigerator should keep a desirable temperature and humidity. Maintenance requirements should also be kept in mind when purchasing a refrigerator. Also, pay attention to the refrigerator's insulation, vapor seal, controls, air circulation, ventilation, and ease of access. A walk-in refrigerator is ideal; but if not feasible from a cost perspective, at least make sure that all parts of the interior can be reached easily. You may also want to check around for used models.),

- Designing tables,

- Wrapping tables,

- Showcases,

- Sinks with a water supply,

- Checkout counter,

- Cash register,

- Display fixtures for flowers and plants,

- Shelving,

- Office equipment (desk, file cabinet, basic office equipment--calculators, staplers, etc.-- and chairs),

- Office supplies (receipts, purchase orders, etc.),

- Delivery van, and

- Miscellaneous supplies (arrangement containers, florist tape, wires, shears, knives, styrofoam, wrapping supplies, watering cans, misters, decorative materials for arrangements, and enclosure cards with envelopes).

Major equipment items may be leased versus bought outright. Also, many flower shops use a centralized delivery service that delivers floral arrangements for several flower shops in the area. You will need to assess which options are most feasible for your business, based on your particular situations.

SERVICES

Flower and gift shops frequently offer amenities such as purchase by credit cards and bank cards, gift wrapping, gift certificates, delivery, in-house credit accounts, and wire services. Many shops also offer various types of floral design classes. Again, you will need to assess your operating environment to determine which services are appropriate for your business.

Wire service connections are very important for the success of a flower business. Customers expect the availability of this service which allows them to send flowers across the country. You should contact the wire services which follow to obtain specifics regarding their operations and criteria for membership.

MAJOR WIRE SERVICES

Florists Transworld Delivery (FTD) 3113 Woodcreek Drive Downers Grove, IL 60515 Phone: 1-800-788-9000 www.FTD.com www.FTDI.com	Teleflora P.O. BOX 60910 Los Angeles, CA 90060-0910 Phone: 1-800-898-7484 www.teleflora.com	Gift Marketing Alliance 599 Sherwood Ave. Suite 107 Satellite Beach, FL 32937 Phone: 800-256-0069 Fax: 321-773-0117 www.giftmarketingalliance.com

SECURITY

Flower and gift shops need to be aware of the theft techniques used by shoplifters and burglars, as well as dishonest employees. The provisions the flower and gift store owner can take to guard against crime are numerous. However, the selection of appropriate preventive measures will be contingent upon the store's operating environment, money available to spend on preventive methods, and insurance requirements.

Preventive measures which can be taken include security mirrors, door and window locks, closed-circuit TV systems, guard dogs, silent alarms, bells that ring when customers walk in, security patrols, fake security cameras, locked display cases for expensive items, an effective screening system for job applicants, watching the cash register, paying attention to inventory levels, and having alert employees, just to mention a few.

FINANCING

Cash flow is very important for a retail firm. If there is insufficient cash coming into the business, the retailer may not be able to pay bills, meet the payroll, handle expenses, and/or take advantage of "special buys" frequently offered by vendors. Many studies show that it is necessary for a retail firm to have sufficient capital to carry the firm for two to three years of operation. Sources of funds are addressed in detail later in this publication.

ADVERTISING

Various marketing strategies are used by floral shops to generate sales. Web site, yellow page advertising, and direct mail seem to be the most common and most effective methods. Other methods include commercial wire transmitting systems for sales to and from other locations.

Various studies pertaining to the floral industry have indicated that a total of 10 percent of sales for advertising and rent combined is a good guideline for determining your advertising budget. The rationale behind combining rent and advertising is that if your rent is higher because of a choice location, you should be able to spend less on advertising. This rule of thumb, of course, is not set in concrete; but it can give you a good starting point for determining how much to allocate for promoting your firm. When just opening your shop, you will have to allocate more for advertising so that your potential customers will be aware of your existence.

Make sure you don't spend all of your advertising dollars on your initial advertising blitz. You will need some forms of continual advertising. You don't want potential customers to think you have gone out of business because they have not seen or heard anything about your business since you first opened. Special promotional activities should occur between major holidays. Flowers are more plentiful and less costly during these periods. This will call upon your ability as a manager to create consumer demand for flowers. This, in fact, is what the floral industry in general has been doing lately. Grandparents' Day, Sweetest Day, and Administrative Assistant's Day are all examples of launching special advertising to create demand.

Major marketing promotions by the floral industry have significantly altered the composition of floral purchasers. Promotions have been so extensive that the market and demand have greatly increased. Subsequently, a significant portion of the floral market has been taken by non-retail florist shops. Grocery stores, department stores, and even gas stations have jumped into the competitive arena.

Some local florists form associations and pool their advertising funds. The pooled monies are used to conduct general advertising campaigns to create demand for flowers and allow the group to buy advertising that they would not be able to afford individually. Talk with other flower shop owners in your area to determine the possibilities.

PERSONNEL

The small retail floral and gift firm cannot generally afford a great number of employees who are specialists or extremely well trained. Therefore, the owner will need to hire employees who are adaptable and can perform various tasks. The employees should be able to convey the atmosphere that you want your store to have and should be well trained in store procedures and merchandise features. The owner will have to put forth a concerted effort to keep employees motivated and to develop a team spirit.

Personnel should always be friendly, knowledgeable about flowers and plants, honest, patient, and willing to give assistance to customers. Customers are "turned off" by pushy, abrasive salespeople and sales personnel who are unable to answer the simplest questions about merchandise. Sales personnel should be trained according to your needs and desires and should project the image you want for your store.

Keeping salespeople happy and motivated to encourage sales requires special effort on the part of the business owner.

GENERAL STRATEGIES FOR STIMULATING SALES

The following strategies are useful for stimulating sales.

- Hold a Christmas "Open House."

- Provide door prizes at women's organizations luncheons or other events.

- Hold an Easter "Open House".

- Provide floral decorations for fashion shows and other community events either free or at a discount. (Make sure you get publicity from the donation.)

- Give presentations to women's organizations, church groups, and garden clubs on topics such as herb gardening, making Christmas arrangements, floral arranging, etc.

- If you have extra room in your store, let civic groups use it in the evening for meetings. This creates goodwill and also encourages sales.

- Hold special sales.

- Appear on television talk shows.

- Keep local newspapers informed about your activities that provide any community service, such as free demonstrations.

- Play an active role in community groups and civic affairs.

- Periodically change your display windows and let prepared floral arrangements disappear, even if they don't sell, so that frequent customers will see new things every time they visit your establishment.

- Periodically send floral arrangements to television talk shows. They will probably say "thank you" to your business on the air, plus it will give you an entree for future publicity coverage.

- Think outside the box and come up with creative exposure strategies appropriate for your operating environment.

SUCCESS TIPS

A few practical success tips are offered in the following list.

- All employees should be knowledgeable of flowers and plants. They should know common as well as botanical names.

- Treat customers buying a single flower with as much courtesy and attention as you would a person placing a $400 order.

- Have all merchandise clearly priced.

- Utilize pictures and visual aids to assist customers in ordering floral designs. This is particularly helpful when selecting and making arrangements for weddings and funerals. You might even consider developing a good rapport with local funeral homes and provide them with visual materials so that customers can simply place the order through the funeral home versus making a trip to your store during their period of bereavement.

- Know customers by name, but don't use endearments such as "honey" or "dearie."

- Keep a card file about the preferences of your regular customers.

- Make sure that every floral arrangement or gift you sell includes a card with your store name, address, phone number, and Web site.

- Consider offering "call services" where you remind customers about birthdays and anniversaries of their loved ones or special friends.

- Consider marketing to corporations customized floral designs and gifts that would be appealing as gifts for their special clients during the holidays or to simply say "thank you."

- Develop an Internet presence.

SUMMATION

Flower and gift shops provide a unique opportunity for the owner to achieve both pleasure and profits while enjoying nature's beautiful flowers and plants. In order to be successful in any business, management knowledge and business planning are crucial. Needless to say, the floral and gift store owner needs to stay abreast of trends in the industry, as well as changes in the environment, economy, and consumer demand. Reading trade journals and belonging to appropriate associations are a "must" for retail selling success. Applicable resources are included in the business resources section of this publication.

The flower shop owner should have a workable selling plan. The selling plan details when items should be promoted through advertising, window displays, and interior decor changes; when the inventory should be peaked; when reorders should no longer be placed; when "markdowns" from regular stock should be taken, and when all merchandise in stock should be sold.

Additionally, in the flower and gift business, the owner must have a knowledge of flowers, green plants, plant nutrition, plant care, insect and disease control, temperature and light requirements, along with artistic and creative flower arranging abilities. An effective combination of all of these factors coupled with enthusiasm, determination, hard work, and a pleasant personality will make you successful in owning and operating a flower and gift shop of your own.

CHAPTER II

Considering the Challenge

THE ENTREPRENEURIAL CHALLENGE

*Business ownership is **a challenging, exhilarating, yet exhausting** way of life. The road to business success is filled with **risk, problems, and pitfalls.** The business owner **must meet these frustrations with perseverance.** An attitude of perseverance, in light of future rewards, helps the business owner to continue the commitment to business. **Perseverance, continual planning, and hard work** enable the business owner to overcome the obstacles inherent in any new venture.*

*__Small business ownership can be a reality for you__. Identify your passion, turn your passion into a profitable venture through planning, and, above all, persevere to create **a business of your own that fulfills your dreams** for the future.*

ON TO THE CHALLENGE....

CONSIDERING THE CHALLENGE

"Like creating the intricate components of a computer system or cultivating a rose garden, pulling together all the elements of a successful small business is an art that requires knowledge, skill, hard work, experience, and much determination." MGLJ

Are you an individualist, an independent-type of person, an adventurer? Are you a risk taker? Do you dislike taking common orders and doing the same thing every day? Do you like the freedom of working independently? Do you like testing your own talents and reaping benefits directly from your personal efforts? Do you desire to use your ideas, abilities, ambitions, aspirations, and initiative to the greatest degree? If you answer "yes" to most of these questions, then maybe you need to consider owning "a business of your own."

Are you are tired of your present work environment or tired of the routine? Do you feel that you are in a rut? Do you feel that your abilities go overlooked? Maybe you simply desire a chance to make more money. Perhaps you think you have a good idea for a business. Are you a displaced homemaker needing to find a way to support yourself? Or do you just have spare time on your hands? If any of these examples fits you, then small business ownership may be the answer allowing you to realize many of your dreams.

There is no question that all people are not qualified to be business owners, nor is there any question that persons who wish to establish a business must depend on their own qualifications and abilities to "make it" or "break it." Going into business is a major decision requiring much commitment.

Business-success potential is highly related to the personal attributes of the business owner. Many studies have been conducted regarding the personal requirements necessary for small business success. Certain common characteristics have been found among successful women who have started businesses. Successful entrepreneurs tend to be decisive and versatile. They follow tasks through to completion. They are self-confident. They are persistent. They have knowledge of the fields in which they start their businesses. They have a strong degree of drive. They are creative and analytical thinkers and have good human relations skills.

AM I DESCRIBING YOU?

Women must realize that they have many inherent talents and abilities which are often taken for granted and have exceptional transferability to the business world. Women have unique talents and skills, instilled during childhood, which may be reflected in their daily life styles and which may be channeled effectively into a business venture. Simple activities normally taken for granted, such as managing the home and managing children, coordinating activities for social organizations, the ability to do ten things at one time, delegating chores and responsibilities at work or at home, organizing a car pool, keeping the boss organized, or being responsible, reliable, and economical are all abilities that frequently go unappreciated and overlooked. They are sometimes even looked down on because they are viewed as being traditional female values or female stereotyping. But, ladies, whether you view yourself as liberated or not, we need to look at ourselves and assess all of these abilities which can easily be transferred into dollars in the business world.

All of us have unique abilities and skills. An in-depth, self-evaluation process will allow you to identify your strongest areas and focus on interests and abilities which could be channeled strategically and successfully into a business venture. This process is a necessity prior to starting a business.

Later in this chapter we proceed with this process and examine your qualities in light of the characteristics common among successful entrepreneurs. But let's first review the research related to entrepreneurial success characteristics.

Individuals contemplating going into business for themselves should be aware of the personal attributes required for success as an entrepreneur. Numerous studies suggest that there are certain personal requirements or personality characteristics which successful small business owner-managers seem to have in common. One such study was conducted by a team of psychologists at Case Western Reserve University. This study utilized tests, questionnaires, and in-depth interviews and examined characteristics of chief executive officers of several successful small businesses. The study resulted in the following profile of the successful entrepreneur:[6]

1. The successful entrepreneur is a moderate risk taker--not a gambler. He [or she] is an adventurer.

2. The successful small business person is decisive and tends to like tight control over decision making.

3. The successful small business person is versatile and tends to strive for competence in many business areas.

4. The successful small business person is a finisher. He [or she] tends to have strong motives to achieve and endure until the completion of a task.

5. The successful small business person is self-confident. He [or she] has a strong belief in his [or her] own capabilities.

6. The successful business person is a benevolent despot, and he [or she] tends to be friendly and willing to listen to the suggestions of subordinates.

Another study of personality characteristics that lead to success in small business was made by H. B. Pickle. He identifies five characteristics he considers significant.[7]

1. Drive--comprised of responsibility, vigor, initiative, persistence, and health;

2. Thinking Ability--comprised of original or creative analytical thinking;

3. Human Relations Ability—comprised of ascendancy, emotional stability, sociability, cautiousness, consideration, cheerfulness, cooperation, and tact;

4. Communications Ability--both oral and written; and

5. Technical Knowledge--comprised of acquired skills developed through study and practical application.

A review of the literature on small business initiation, ownership, and management leads to the conclusion that there are various personal attributes necessary for success in entrepreneurship. The Small Business Administration (SBA), the governmental agency which assists small businesses, identifies certain personal attributes as being necessary for entrepreneurial success. Included in the list are the following 18 characteristics and abilities:

- Ability and understanding of others,

- Willingness to take a chance,

- Ability to withstand stress,

- Ability to take over when the going gets rough,

- Honesty in business relationships,

- Selling skills,

- Spirit to meet competition,

- Ability to keep abreast of new technology in the field, as well as environmental changes,

- Initiative and leadership abilities,

- High capability for organizing,

- Industriousness and capability to work long hours,

- Ability to make and guide accurate decisions,

- Perseverance (not discouraged by obstacles),

- Desire to get ahead with a high level of energy,

- Ability to understand customers and their desires,

- Ability to adapt to change,

- Innovativeness, and

- Ability to inspire and direct or motivate[8]

There has been considerable interest in the nature of the entrepreneur for many years, but interest in the female entrepreneur has surfaced only recently. This interest has been generated by the recognition that the entrepreneur is a central figure in economic activity. However, relatively little research has been done on the female entrepreneur; and much of the research conducted has been based on perceptual responses rather than objective measurements. Hornaday and Aboud made attempts to develop and identify objective tests which were valid and which would not require administration by a psychologist. They found that the achievement scale of the Edwards Personal Preference Schedule and the Support, Independence, and Leadership scales of the Gordon Survey of Interpersonal Values held promise for distinguishing between entrepreneurs.[9]

Decarlo and Lyons conducted research using Hornaday and Aboud's findings as a guide. They compared selected personal characteristics of minority and non-minority female entrepreneurs. The characteristics on which noticeable differences occurred were:[10]

- Age of entrepreneur--The minority females were somewhat older than their non-minority counterparts.

- Age at the time of starting a business--The minority females reported they started their businesses at a later age than non-minority females.

- Previous entrepreneurial effort--Almost twice as many minority females as non-minority females reported that their current businesses were not their first entrepreneurial effort.

- Marriage rate--A greater proportion of the non-minority females reported never having been married. This is contrary to the 1975 Census data that reported half again as many black women as white women had never been married.

- Educational experience--A greater proportion of non-minority females reported having graduated from both high school and college. Both groups reported a higher education level than the Census had reported for all females in 1975. According to the Census, only 64 percent of all females over age 25 had completed four years of high school or more. The minority females, however, reported being more active than non-minority females in extracurricular activities and were responsible for personally financing their college educations.

- Acceptance regimentation--A much greater percentage of minority females reported a willingness to accept regimentation than did the non-minority females. This may reflect the fact that female entrepreneurs represent a distinct minority in the business world.

- Means of starting a business--The minority women were much more likely than the non-minority women to have started their businesses alone than with a partner.

When non-minority female entrepreneurs were compared to minority female entrepreneurs on the nine scales of achievement, autonomy, aggression, support, conformity, recognition, independence, benevolence, and leadership, it was found that significant differences existed on six of the nine scales. The non-minority females placed a higher value on the scales of achievement, support, recognition, and independence; whereas, the minority females placed a higher value on the conformity and benevolence scales.[11]

John Mancuso has studied a group of 300 entrepreneurs for several years. He has concluded that the typical successful entrepreneur can be described as follows:[12]

- The entrepreneur is the first-born child in his or her family.

- The entrepreneur is married, with a supportive spouse.

- The entrepreneur began his or her first company at the age of 30 or so.

- Entrepreneurial tendencies manifested themselves during the teenage years.

- The level of education varies among entrepreneurs. The technical entrepreneur often has a master's degree. The typical entrepreneur probably has at least a high school and probably a college degree.

- The entrepreneur's primary motivation for going into business for herself or himself is a psychological inability to work for anyone else.

- The entrepreneur's personality developed mainly in interaction with his or her father's personality.

- The successful entrepreneur is often lucky.

- The entrepreneur seeks advice, if it is needed, from other entrepreneurs, consultants, and college professors.

- Entrepreneurs and money providers are often in conflict.

- The entrepreneur is essentially a doer, not a planner.

- The entrepreneur assumes moderate risks, not large or small ones.

Until recently, the world of the entrepreneur was almost entirely male. This remains true; but women are entering this world more frequently than in the past, now that the opportunities are more readily available and societal values have shifted so that it is acceptable for women to want to run their own businesses. James Schreier recently studied Milwaukee female entrepreneurs who created enterprises in "non-female" businesses (that is, he ignored Mary's Beauty Shop). He judged them by the characteristics just cited (Mancuso's study) and found the following differences.[13]

1. A stronger tendency toward self-employment in the family: 70 percent of male entrepreneurs came from a family headed by an entrepreneur; 93 percent of Schreier's female entrepreneurs did.

2. Seventy-two percent of the female entrepreneurs liked school; whereas, the male entrepreneurs (non-technical) did not like it.

3. Male entrepreneurs become entrepreneurs because they cannot work for others, as evidenced by prior job history; 50 percent of the female entrepreneurs liked working for others in previous jobs.

4. More female entrepreneurs than male ones are divorced or single.

5. Entrepreneurial behavior manifested itself later in women but mainly because of lack of opportunity. For example, some city newspapers would not hire female paper carriers.

Entrepreneurs are, of course, leaders in their own businesses, so that it is significant to examine theories pertaining to successful leadership. The following section explores two leadership trait surveys. The original survey conducted in 1948 by Stogdill, a well-known authority on leadership, reviews 24 trait studies of leadership characteristics.[14]

Successful Leadership Traits

Identified traits for successful leadership include the following:

Personality, Intelligence and Ability

In reviewing the 1948 and 1970 lists of personality characteristics, it is noted that characteristics with uniformly positive findings, which appear only in the 1948 list, are **adaptability** and **strength of conviction**. Those that appear only in the 1970 list are **adjustment, aggressiveness, independence, objectivity, resourcefulness**, and **tolerance of stress**. Characteristics that appear with positive findings in both 1948 and 1970 lists are **alertness, originality, personal integrity**, and **self-confidence**. The research consistently reports that leaders are characterized by **superior judgement, decisiveness, knowledge**, and **fluency of speech**.

Task-Oriented Characteristics

Both surveys indicate that leaders are characterized by a high need for achievement and responsibility. They tend to be very task-oriented, dependable, persistent, have initiative, drive, and are very enterprising.

Physical Characteristics

Results of recent research suggest that leaders tend to be endowed with an abundant reserve of energy, stamina, and the ability to maintain a high rate of physical activity.

Social Characteristics

Leaders tend to be quite active in various social activities and get along well with others. Personality traits have been found to differentiate leaders from followers, successful from unsuccessful leaders and high-level from lower-level leaders. When considered singly, the characteristics hold very little predictive or diagnostic possibilities. In combination, however, they can generate personality dynamics advantageous to the person seeking responsibilities of leadership. Examining personality as this author has, does not imply advocating a return to the trait approach to leadership in which personality variables were treated in somewhat of an isolated fashion, suggesting that each trait acted independently to determine leadership effects. The author has modified the situation approach, with traits considered in conjunction with the situation.

When Stogdill analyzed 124 studies on leadership, he found that patterns of leadership traits differ, depending on the situation. According to Stogdill, "If there are general traits which characterize leaders, the patterns of such traits are likely to vary with the leadership requirements of different situations."[15]

The various research results previously cited can generally be summarized into two categories: **characteristics** and **personal requirements** for success in small business management.

Characteristics of Successful Small Business Managers

The following list succinctly delineates characteristics that typify successful small business managers.

1. A great sense of independence and a desire to be independent of outside control,

2. A strong sense of enterprise which lends itself to a desire to use their ideas, abilities, ambitions, aspirations, and initiatives to the greatest degree,

3. Taking their families into consideration,

4. Entrance into small business by chance rather than design,

5. Guarding their time,

6. A limited formal education, and

7. An expectation for quick results.

Professional Requirements for Success in Small Business

Contained in the list that follows are professional requirements for successful small business managers.

1. Sensitivity to internal and external changes,

2. Ability to react quickly to those changes,

3. Ability to obtain accurate and useful operating and marketing information,

4. Effective use of human resources,

5. Obtaining sufficient investment capital,

6. Effective compliance with laws,

7. Thorough understanding of the peculiarities of size,

8. Gathering industry information and keeping informed, and

9. Handling "red tape" effectively.

Motivation of Entrepreneurs

One can also look at entrepreneurs in terms of motivation theories. According to Maslow's hierarchy of needs theory, individuals move from one level to the next only after lower needs have been satisfied or nearly satisfied. Accordingly, after considerable satisfaction of basic physiological needs (hunger, thirst, etc.), the typical person would next pursue safety, social, self-esteem, and finally, self-actualization needs. Research conducted by Swayne and Tucker indicates that entrepreneurs differ from the normal population. According to them, entrepreneurs seem to be strongly motivated by self-esteem and have a fairly low requirement for love, social, physiological, and safety needs.[16]   Going hand in hand with Maslow's theory and their findings regarding entrepreneurs, the true entrepreneur will continue to start new ventures, and new businesses and accept new challenges even though he [or she] is financially well-off. He [or she] continues to strive for self-actualization through new and exciting ventures; and even though the finer things in life are enjoyed, the thrust is toward continuing entrepreneurial endeavors.[17]

David McClelland has devoted great efforts to examine a person's need for achievement. He [or she] has developed a need for achievement (nAch) index which can be an excellent indicator of entrepreneurial potential. Also related to nAch and entrepreneurship is the need for power (nPow) and the need for affiliation (nAff).[18]

Successful entrepreneurs also have a strong belief in their abilities to control their own lives. They do not feel that other people or conditions in the external environment can keep them from doing what they want to accomplish. Julian Rotter has pioneered the development of measures for an internal-external (I-E) scale. His method involved forced choices between pairs of statements presented to a subject for evaluation. Possible scores range from 0 (extremely internal) to 23 (extremely external). Studies indicate that entrepreneurs score lower than 7 while the general population scores higher on the I-E rating. The conclusion appears to be that believing in one's ability to be successful is very important in determining entrepreneurial potential.[19]

More women than ever before are considering entrepreneurship as a career option; however, the majority of the women in the work force still think in terms of being the employee rather than the employer. Realizing that all women will not make good entrepreneurs, if you think you have the ability, a good business idea, or just the desire and determination to utilize your abilities to the fullest extent, you may want to consider entrepreneurship as a career option. Entrepreneurship is indeed risky and complicated and requires much dedication. It would be remiss not say that women also face many obstacles that can make the entrepreneurial road even more difficult than working a 9-5 job or staying home. Women frequently encounter credit procurement obstacles, financial barricades, and negative attitudes from male counterparts; often lack business experience; and suffer from a lack of role models and a peer support base, just to mention a few.

Even if you know you have a great business idea but realize that you may not have the personal qualities to make the idea become a reality by way of a business venture, do not abandon the thought of ownership yet. There are many entrepreneurial success qualities that can be learned and developed. To achieve business success, other qualities can be obtained by joining with other individuals who have the skills, abilities, expertise, or characteristics that you may be lacking. Remember, a business idea can only become a successful business with careful planning and the implementation of appropriate business knowledge, coupled with the personal characteristics necessary for small business success.

Let's now assess your skills, abilities, talents, and strengths. We all have many attributes which could be very beneficial in the world of entrepreneurship, but many of these positive traits often go overlooked and unidentified. Take time to identify all of your strengths. Your strong points could include special talents, knowledge, past experience, tenacity, determination, levelheadedness, logical thinking, standing up well under stress, good communication skills, creativity, artistry, etc.

LIST YOUR STRENGTHS

(Don't be modest)

Just as you may have many personality characteristics that could help you succeed as a business owner, you may also have weaknesses which could eventually lead to entrepreneurial demise. Some of these weaknesses might include a tendency not to complete tasks you start, being more comfortable as a follower and disliking leadership responsibilities, being gullible or too kindhearted, hating to hurt someone else's feelings even though you suffer the negative consequences, being unorganized, hating details, etc. Remember, some tendencies or traits may not have been considered weaknesses before, but need to be examined now in light of the immense personal requirements necessary for success as a business owner and leader.

LIST YOUR WEAKNESSES
(Own up to all of them.)

Now, go back and review your strengths and weaknesses. Compare your strengths and your alterable weaknesses with the characteristics common among successful entrepreneurs. Do you have significant weaknesses? If so, can most of them be positively changed? Do you think you have what it takes for entrepreneurial success?

Before embarking on any new enterprise, potential entrepreneurs need to be in touch with themselves, their desires and their personal objectives, as well as their strengths and weaknesses. The following format should help you become more aware of your individual goals and assist you in further assessing your personal qualities relative to the characteristics common among successful female entrepreneurs.

LIFE PLANNING

PURPOSE: TO SET AT LEAST TWO CLEAR GOALS FOR YOUR LIFE, TO SPECIFY PLANS OF ACTION TO REACH THOSE GOALS AND TO HELP YOU DETERMINE IF YOU HAVE A GENUINE INTEREST IN ENTREPRENEURSHIP.

Life Line

Use the following line to represent your life from beginning to end. Put a check mark on the line to indicate where you are now.

BIRTH_____**DEATH**

Address such questions as:

- What was the happiest year or period in your life?
- What was the turning point in your life?
- What was the lowest point in your life?
- Was there an event in your life when you demonstrated great courage?
- Was there a time of great grief?

- What peak experiences have you had? What things do you want to start doing at this point in your life?
- Was there a time when you were very enterprising?

Reflect on your feelings represented by the line before and after the check mark. What does this tell you about who you are and what you want out of life?

Typical Day

A circle will be used to depict how you spend a typical day. Divide the circle into four quarters using dotted lines. Each slice represents six hours. Now, estimate how many hours or parts of an hour you spend on each of the following areas on a typical day: SLEEP, SCHOOL, WORK, WITH FRIENDS--socializing, playing sports, etc., WITH FAMILY, ALONE-- thinking, playing, reading, watching television, CHORES, MISCELLANEOUS PASTIMES, ETC.

MY TYPICAL DAY

Are you satisfied with the relative sizes of your slices?

How Would You Like Your Ideal Day To Look?

Ideally, how big would you want each slice to be? Draw your ideal pie.

MY IDEAL DAY

Realistically, is there anything you can do to begin to change the size of some of your slices to the desired sizes?

SHORT-TERM AND LONG-TERM GOALS

What type of business do you see yourself running? What type of facility? How many employees do you have? How many customers or clients on a daily and monthly basis? What type of revenue and profit do you expect to realize in the beginning as well as subsequent years? What type of lifestyle do you want to create? At the same time, consider how much time will be required to achieve your goals. How much work will be required? Will your family be supportive, or will conflicts arise? Sometimes you even need to consider subconscious jealousy and/or competition from your spouse or significant other and the negative repercussions. You may also run into the double bind of taking so much of your time to make your business a success and achieving the income that comes along with success that, when you realize the fruits of your labor and have extra money to enjoy life through vacations and family fun, you don't have time to really enjoy yourself because you have to constantly devote more time to keeping the business successful, and/or you find that your mind is constantly on the business. This is one of the drawbacks of success. In essence, when you consider your goals, you may want to consciously limit your growth, based on your values, priorities, and personal situation. This is a major consideration that should be addressed at the initiation of a business.

Make sure that you set realistic goals and expectations of yourself and your business. If your goals are too high, you will quickly find yourself discouraged and frustrated. Conservative business goals will allow you to be exuberant and more motivated when you do better than you anticipated. Make sure you have prioritized your goals, assessed all drawbacks, and know what really makes you happy. Consider all of these factors as we proceed to the next section concerning the selection of a business that's right for you. But first take some time and write down your short-term and long-term goals. Make sure you attach a specific time frame to each goal.

SHORT-TERM GOALS

LONG-TERM GOALS

SELF-AWARENESS

This section involves looking at yourself by way of developing a coat of arms as seen on the following page. This should help you address the following considerations: WHAT AM I DOING WITH MY LIFE? AM I JUST REACTING TO OTHERS, OR AM I IN CONTROL OF THE DIRECTION OF MY LIFE? IS MY LIFE MAKING A DIFFERENCE? AM I JUST SETTLING FOR WHATEVER COMES MY WAY?

Answer each of the questions below by drawing in the appropriate area on the coat of arms on the following page. Use pictures, designs, or symbols. Do not use words except in area six.

1. What do you regard as your greatest personal achievement to date?

2. What do you regard as your family's greatest achievement?

3. What do you regard as your own greatest personal failure to date?

4. What is something you are striving to become or to be?

5. What one thing would you want to accomplish by the time you are 85?

6. What is the personal motto by which you live?

COAT OF ARMS

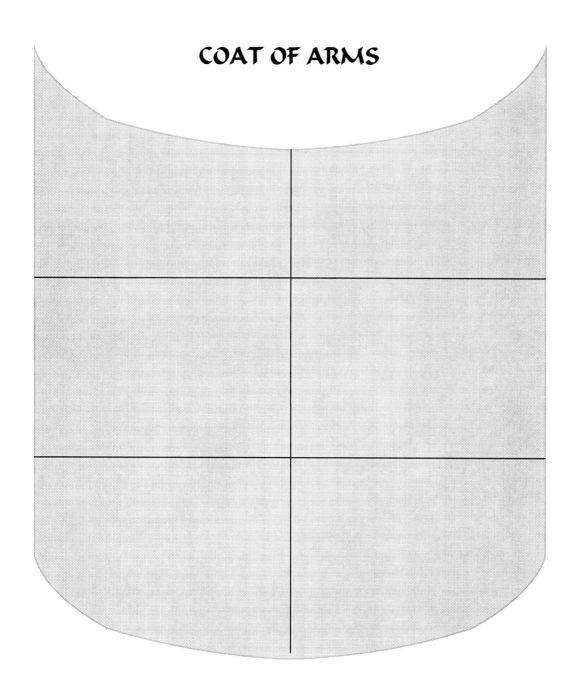

What would you most like to accomplish in your lifetime?

Write for two minutes without stopping. (Make sure to reflect on all aspects of your life, including family, finances, and the physical, social, spiritual, love, and intellectual components of your life.)

You will need to thoroughly assess your likes and dislikes about work. The total responsibility of the business rests on the shoulders of the business owner. The business owner will need to be prepared to do all of the tasks required to keep the business going. Even though you may hire people to do the tasks you might dislike, such as bookkeeping, there will come a time when you will have to pitch in and help or do it all, either because of employee absence from work or because of cost-cutting considerations. In the beginning, you may be working with limited capital and may have to do everything yourself. Make sure that you are mentally prepared to cope with having to perform "hated" tasks.

LIKES AND DISLIKES ABOUT JOBS/WORK

LIKES	DISLIKES
1.	1.
2.	2.
3.	3.
4.	4.
5.	5.
6.	6.
7.	7.

REVIEW

Look back over your responses and address the following:

1. What do you want in your future?

2. You may find that priorities for your desires and goals have emerged. Set dates for accomplishments. You may have discovered hidden interests. Include the type of business you may want to start if business ownership is part of your desires.

3. How do your personal characteristics rate compared to those of successful entrepreneurs?

HOW DO YOU PLAN TO GET THERE?

1. What resources do you have to help you achieve these goals?

2. What training or experience is needed to achieve these goals?

3. What things do you want or need to start doing less? More?

4. Are your life goals oriented toward owning and operating your own business? What type? What leads you to your conclusions?

SELECTING THE TYPE OF BUSINESS TO ENTER

Even though the number of female-owned businesses is increasing, the success of these ventures is not guaranteed. Successful ventures can only occur with careful planning and the execution of good business and management principles and practices, coupled with the existence of necessary personal factors on the part of the business owner.

Approximately 55 percent of all small business failures are due partially, if not entirely, to the lack of managerial ability and experience.[17] Certainly, therefore, managerial knowledge and ability are necessary for success in small business. This publication will provide the basic knowledge necessary for starting and operating a small business. It should be noted that management ability includes the personal requirements necessary for success which can often be overlooked when evaluating the reason a certain business is successful or unsuccessful. Entrepreneurial success depends significantly on the existence of strong personal entrepreneurial requirements and not business knowledge alone. This publication, therefore, also presents significant information concerning entrepreneurial characteristics as well as managerial knowledge. The information presented allows the reader to identify a type of business venture and then conduct an analysis to determine whether that possible business is, in fact, a feasible venture and whether it has a chance for success. At the same time, the information also allows the reader to develop a business plan for the venture.

BACKGROUND

There is not any consistent definition for a small business. Some of the small business literature uses a definition such as a firm having a name, an owner, and one or more workers other than the owner. Using such a broad definition, approximately 95 percent of all businesses can be considered small. The Small Business Administration (SBA), the governmental agency directing efforts toward small business, defines a small business as a business independently owned and operated, and not dominant in its field. The SBA goes further to categorize firms as being small by way of certain criteria such as number of employees and dollar volume of business. One really has to develop a feel for what a small business is. Generally, if one is starting a new business, it can be assumed that it will be considered small initially. Small business offers many benefits. Small firms tend:

1. to be more in touch with employees, thereby encouraging better employee relations;

2. to be more in touch with customers and can provide more personal service;

3. to provide almost half of all jobs;

4. to help insure competition;

5. to provide jobs for the disadvantaged and ethnic groups;

6. to help expand the economy;

7. to provide workers and owners with wider learning experiences;

8. to provide personal rewards (i.e., financial security or wealth, personal satisfaction, and, what is considered a major advantage by many, independence).

The problems encountered by small businesses are many. The disadvantages and pitfalls of small business include the following:

1. Fewer opportunities to make costly mistakes (One major mistake, such as purchasing the wrong inventory, can cause failure.),

2. Inadequate funds to employ managerial assistance or consulting help,

3. Shortage of working capital,

4. Poor record-keeping systems,

5. Lack of effective selling techniques,

6. No marketing research,

7. Inability to cope with growth problems,

8. Lack of experience of many entrepreneurs,

9. Poor location selection,

10. Too much inventory, particularly the wrong kind,

11. Excessive purchase of fixed assets, such as elaborate buildings when first starting,

12. Poor credit-granting policies,

13. Unwarranted personal expenditures;

14. Unplanned expansions.

Given the many pitfalls of small business, the failure rate of small businesses is extraordinarily high. Half of the businesses started each year fail. Half of the businesses that fail do so during the first five years of operation. Nine out of ten failures are traceable to managerial inexperience and incompetence. Other reasons for business failures include too little capital, poor organization, obsolescence of service or product, obsolescence of equipment, poor personnel practices, and inappropriate personal characteristics.

At this point, you should have determined that you have or can develop the personal characteristics required for success as an entrepreneur and that you truly want to take the entrepreneurial challenge. We now need to put those success traits into action and start developing your business.

Types of Businesses

By virtue of the fact that you are reading this book, you have probably already decided that you want to start a flower shop. However, the type of business you enter will be influenced by your personal value system, education, training, financial ability, and family situation, as well as by your particular interests and desires.

Small businesses can be categorized into six types:

1. retailing,
2. service,
3. wholesaling,
4. research and development,
5. consulting, and
6. manufacturing.

You must start with a business idea and develop your business or venture from there. Before making a preliminary analysis of the market, production, or financial aspects of your venture, you must be able to describe and define your business concept. An idea for a business must address a need of an identified market which is presently not satisfied and, at the same time, be innovative enough to attract people to your product or service as opposed to the competition. It is important to be innovative enough to attract customers; but if your service or product is too unusual, it may take too long for people to accept it. Consequently, your business will fail while you attempt to make people aware of the need for your product or service. Realize that the type of business you enter will be influenced by your personal value system, education, training, financial ability, and your family situation, as well as by your particular interests and desires. As you attempt to think of the type of business you may want to start, reflecting on the following list of some specific types of businesses may trigger a few thoughts. The list is presented only to serve as a "bouncing board."

Antique shop
Art show promotion
Artwork (sales)
Baby-sitting service (day/night)
Bake shop
Beauty services
Business consulting
Calligraphy instruction
Candy-making business
Caning chairs
Child care
Classes and instruction in your skill areas
Casket rental
Cleaning services
Clown birthday party service
Computer sales
Consignment shop (clothier, baby items, furniture)
Craft shop
Dietary bakery
Disco
Designer clothier (boutique, rentals, re-sale)
Dinners to go (elegant take-out dinners or healthy dinners)
Elder care
Errand service
Fabric sales and design

Financial services
Flower shop
Flowers and plants (preservation services, arrangement, rentals)
Food service (delivery, different homemade items, catering)
Frame shop (sales, framing, unique design)
Fur sales
Furniture sales and rental
Gifts (sales, buying, wrapping, and delivery service)
Gourmet coffee and tea shop
Greenhouses (sales, installation, consultation on use)
Herb shop
Instruction (piano, gymnastics, dancing, etc.)
Jewelry store
Lawn care service (grass cutting, plant, flower and shrub planting and care)
Legal courier service
Maid service
Manufacturing
Monogram service
Movie club
Nannies for rent
Oriental rugs
Pet grooming and care
Potato restaurant
Public relations firm
Roller skating rink
Roommate finder service
Sale-by-owner listing (listing of homes for sale by owners)
Salads-only restaurant
Sick child care site
Silk flower rental service
Self-service pet wash (like a car wash for animals)
Security patrol service
Telephone answering service
Secretarial service
Temporary personnel service
Tennis/Racquetball club
Tourist services
Video gameroom

In selecting a business, you should address the following major questions:

1. What type of business do you think you might want to enter? Why?

2. Exactly what products and/or services should be sold?

3. Who will be the primary customer groups for your product or service?

4. What are the eventual uses for your product or service by the customer?

5. Why will customers want to buy your product or service? (Ask yourself questions which identify the key benefits or advantages of your product or service to the customer, lower price, better quality, etc.)

6. What in fact is your total product? (List everything you will be offering to your customers, not only the physical.)

ASSESSING YOUR MONETARY REQUIREMENTS

The question that is probably running through your mind is how much money is needed to get the business started and keep it operating? This question cannot be addressed without first taking an in-depth look at the total venture you're considering. All of the information obtained can then be compiled in a business plan format. Below you will find factors that will need to be addressed and considered in determining start-up and operating costs. This information is presented in brief in this section. It is presented at this time so that you will be conscious of significant cost centers as we begin working on preparing a business plan for your venture. Capital requirements will be addressed in a more detailed worksheet format as a part of the business plan preparation process in Chapter III.

The amount of money you will need to start your business depends on many factors. The following are major factors you need to take into consideration in determining your monetary requirements:

- the type of business being established,

- the location of the business,

- the sales volume anticipated,

- how quickly the sales volume desired can be obtained,

- whether you buy or lease the facilities in which the business will be operating,

- how extensive the product line is,

- whether the business will operate on a cash basis or extend credit,

- how much money the entrepreneur has to invest in the business,

- how much legal assistance is needed,

- the cost of preparing the business facility for use,

- the cost of store fixtures and equipment,

- the amount and cost of the beginning inventory,

- the cost of establishing an accounting system and the forms required,

- the cost of personnel,

- the cost of delivering merchandise to customers and inventory to the business,

- the cost of licenses and permits,

- the cost of utilities,

- the cost of insurance,

- advertising expenses, and

- the amount of money deposited in a reserve fund to take care of business and personal expenses until your business turns a profit.

All of these factors have been taken into consideration in the preparation of the cost worksheets that follow. As we work on the preparation of your business plan, you will be able to insert certain costs when they are considered.

START-UP COSTS

Start-up costs include all of the expenses your business will incur in preparation for opening. Major cost areas are presented below; however, you will need to alter the sample form, based on the specifics of your business. Some of the expenses listed will be one-time only costs or expenses you incur once a year. Other expenses will occur monthly.

BUSINESS ORGANIZATIONAL EXPENSES	MONTHLY	YEARLY
Start-up inventory		
Facility costs		
Decorating and remodeling		
Furniture		
Professional and legal fees		
Franchise fee, if applicable		
Licenses and permits		
Telephone installation		
Telephone services		
Telephone answering service		
Insurance		
Personnel		
Deposits for utilities		
Installation of fixtures		
TOTAL		
ADVERTISING AND PROMOTIONAL EXPENSES		
Business cards		
Mailers, posters, ads		
Business logo design		
Signs (outdoor)		
Bags		
Other		
TOTAL		
OFFICE OPERATING EXPENSES		
Stationery		
Invoice forms		
Purchase order forms		
Computer		
Pens, pencils, misc.		
Tables & Equipment		
Other		
TOTAL		

FURNITURE AND FIXTURES		
Desks and chairs		
Filing cabinets		
Wastebaskets		
Safe		
Copying machine		
Adding machine		
Storage shelves		
Cabinets		
Computers & Technology		
Office furniture		
Lighting		
Display cases		
Refrigerated display cases		
TOTAL		
BUSINESS VEHICLE		
REAL ESTATE		
EQUIPMENT		
OWNER'S LIVING EXPENSES		
Home mortgage payments or rent		
Food		
Home repair and maintenance		
Outstanding debts (Credit cards, etc,)		
Loans		
Entertainment		
Education		
Auto and repair		
Furniture		
Clothing		
Travel		
Taxes		
Utilities		
Medical expenses		
Insurance costs		
Other		
TOTAL		
TOTAL PERSONAL EXPENSES		
Subtract outside income yet to be obtained while running the business.		
TOTAL PERSONAL EXPENSES TO BE COVERED BY THE BUSINESS		

EVALUATING YOUR MONETARY REQUIREMENTS

Prior to approaching a lending institution or investors for assistance in funding your business, you will need to make sure you have the answers to the following questions:

1. How much money do you need?

2. What exactly do you need the money for? Some specific reasons for needing money include buying equipment, supplies, renting space, salaries, money to meet financial obligations to suppliers, etc.

3. What collateral do you have? What do you or your business own which can be offered as security for money received?

4. When do you need the money?

5. How long do you need the money?

6. Can you afford the cost of the money?

7. Where can you find the money? (Make sure you have backups in place.)

REMEMBER, IT IS BETTER TO OVERESTIMATE THAN UNDERESTIMATE YOUR FINANCIAL REQUIREMENTS!!

The answers to all of these questions and other major business considerations should be summarized in a coherent, precise written format. This information constitutes a business plan and is discussed in the following chapter.

"There is no fast, challenge-free road to success.

You have to take it one step at a time, overcome one

challenge at a time, and turn the challenges into

opportunities to determine your inner strength."

M.G.L.J.

CHAPTER III

The Business Plan

"Three Critical Keys to Entrepreneurial Success:

PASSION, PLANNING, AND PERSEVERANCE."

M.G.L.J.

THE BUSINESS PLAN

A business plan is a report written by the initiator of a business which describes the venture in detail--WHAT business you are in, WHO will be active in it, WHY you believe it will be successful, and HOW you intend to implement your plans. The business plan should be prepared with great care and thought and should be concise, readable, well written, and substantive.

From an internal perspective, the business plan forces the business owner to write down all of his or her thoughts and researched data pertaining to the business. Many considerations would go unaddressed, and many thoughts and ideas would never be captured again if it were not for the business plan. The business plan is also crucial because it serves as a checklist and timetable for accomplishing stated objectives.

Externally, the business plan is used to attract financial as well as human resources. Lending institutions and investors want to be able to examine your organized plans to determine if your venture has merit and whether it warrants their investment. The business plan can also be used to attract key personnel and business partners, as well as serve as a means to communicate to others what your business is about. Even many small business consulting firms and assistance offices will ask you for a business plan prior to rendering any type of service. A GOOD BUSINESS PLAN IS CRUCIAL!

A good business plan will consist of, but is not limited to, the following major informational areas.

The Business

- Detailed description of the business including name, location, business goals and objectives, industry information and assessment, economic trends, etc.;

- Description of the product (services and/or goods), potential of product line, technology, and possible advances;

- Description of the marketing plan, including target market, marketing strategies, channels of distribution, market size and share, market potential, pricing strategy, and promotion;

- Assessment of competition;

- Management, covering such areas as key personnel, names of accountants, lawyers, consultants, organizational structure, experience of key personnel, educational background and experience;

- Legal structure, describing the proprietorship, partnership, or corporation;

- Personnel, listing personnel requirements, position descriptions, labor trends, and compensation;

- Facilities and equipment;

- Sources of supply;

- Critical risks and problems;

- Economic trends; and

- Strategies for the future.

Financial Data

- Capital equipment,

- Sources of funds,

- Balance sheet,

- Break-even analysis,

- Income projections or profit-loss statement,

- Pro forma cash flow,

- Uses of funds, and

- Desired funding.

Supporting Documents

- Resumes of key personnel,

- Personal financial statements,

- Credit reports,

- Letters of reference,

- Copies of leases,

- Contracts,

- Legal documents,

- Drawings,

- Photographs,

- Articles, and

- Any additional pertinent information.

The following worksheets are provided to help you organize your thoughts regarding your business. The remaining format of this publication will present crucial information necessary for starting a retail flower business followed by questions for you to address. The summarization of the answers to these questions will be important components of your business plan. Upon completion of this publication, you should have your business plan in good order.

Now that you have a feel for what is included in a completed business plan, continue reading the next chapter on start-up costs. It will become obvious that in order to fill in most of these blanks, substantial investigatory work will have to be done on your part. In fact, these blanks will need to be filled in, as well as the questions answered from the previous section on your financial needs, before you near the completion of your plan. All of these questions need to be kept in mind throughout the business plan preparation process.

BUSINESS PLAN WORKSHEETS

The importance of a well-conceived business plan cannot be stressed enough. The business plan outline covers the major topics to be considered in the planning process. Experience has revealed that most mistakes or failures of businesses occur not from bad information, but from a lack of information. The business plan, among other things, helps you to determine if you have sufficient information, capital, and customers to initiate your venture. As stated earlier, the business plan is of immensely important in requesting a bank loan or any form of financing or assistance. Even an advertising consultant will ask to see your business plan before attempting to map out an advertising program for your firm. These worksheets are designed in such a way that you can simply fill in the blanks and have a basic narrative for all business plan components. As you proceed with this manual, insert the appropriate information in the spaces provided. Also, make sure you insert appropriate amounts on your cost sheets. Upon completion of the publication, you should have completed your business plan and have it ready to be typed.

BUSINESS PLAN

NAME OF THE BUSINESS: _____

Be sure the name is distinctive, will stick in the minds of your customers or clients, and accurately describes the nature of your business. Also check to make sure that no one else is using the name or a very similar name, particularly in the same industry.

Check with your state trademark office and register your business name. This is usually not very expensive, but be sure to include the cost on your cost sheet. You may also want to register your business name and logo, that is, the symbol that you use to identify your business, with the Federal Trademark Office. If you are having trouble coming up with a name, don't belabor the point. A good name will probably come to you as you continue your investigatory work into the industry.

LOCATION: In light of the selected target market and after reflecting on many major

location considerations, _____ will be strategically
                                    (name of business)

located at:_____.

This location was selected because. . . . .

Take time to thoroughly assess your location options and reflect on the information presented in this section of the manual. Make sure you have considered such factors as the pros and cons of a post office box, your business image, operating out of a home office, and accessibility to your target market, as well as cost factors. (See Chapter VI.)

TELEPHONE: _____

Make sure you have a business listing in the phone book even if you are operating out of the home. Your accessibility by phone is very important. If you cannot afford a secretary, use an answering service. Avoid answering machines if at all possible. They are a turn-off to most people. Don't forget to include your business telephone and answering service costs on your cost sheets.

STATEMENT OF PURPOSE AND NATURE OF BUSINESS:

_____

_____

_____

_____

WHAT IS THE PURPOSE OF YOUR BUSINESS? WHAT MARKET ARE YOU AIMING FOR? WHY ARE YOU IN BUSINESS? THIS SHOULD BE A SUCCINCT STATEMENT PERTAINING TO WHAT YOUR BUSINESS IS ALL ABOUT.

EXAMPLE: "A BUSINESS OF YOUR OWN" is a multi-faceted service firm established to assist women in starting and managing small businesses. "A BUSINESS OF YOUR OWN" specializes in business start-up publications and auxiliary services to assist the female small business owner and aspiring owner. "A BUSINESS OF YOUR OWN" publications range from general start-up manuals to more specific manuals with information about starting particular businesses. "A BUSINESS OF YOUR OWN'S" goal is to assist women in pulling together the intricate components necessary to make their small businesses successful.

Industry Overview: Examine the industry your business is in from national, regional, and local standpoints. Include a narrative which will address historical and concrete growth projections along with the number of local and national firms. Discuss how your venture fits into the industry context and indicate factors that will give your business the competitive edge in the marketplace, based on industry information. Much industry information can be obtained from the local library, trade associations and trade publications, and from Web sites. Be sure to check the appendix of this manual for useful informational sources.

Form of Ownership: _____ is a _____.
                              name of business   form of ownership

Discuss the form of legal ownership (proprietorship, partnership, or corporation) your business will use and why. (See Chapter V.)

Marketing: Discuss your **target market**. Use results from your research to justify the appropriateness of your market. Cite published information which support your target market selection. Discuss in detail your "total product," including auxiliary services, packaging, warranties, delivery service, repairs, installation, guarantees, etc. Detail your promotion plans for attracting customers or clients, penetrating your target market, and getting repeat customers. Again, do not forget to insert all of your marketing costs on the cost sheets. Discuss how your product will be **distributed** and/or how services will be performed. What type of market penetration do you hope to obtain and when? What is the **pricing** structure for your products and services? Make sure you can show legitimate justification for all of your business decisions, and make sure you are being consistent with your image and product positioning. (See Chapter IV.)

The selected target market for _____
                              (name of business)

is _____. This market was determined
                    (target market)

to be appropriate after conducting marketing research. _____ individuals were surveyed
                                                        (# people)

for the purpose of _____ and to

determine if originally identified target market would be receptive to the business idea. The

survey findings are presented in the appendix.

The product of _____ is presently in the
               (name of business)

_____ stage of development. The product has many
(introduction, growth, maturity)

strengths, including _____. In spite of the many strengths

of the business's products/services, certain weaknesses have been identified. These

weaknesses are as follows: _____. The identified

weaknesses will be overcome by _____
(action to be taken)

_____.

To inform and persuade customers/clients to patronize _____,
(name of business)

a varied promotional strategy will be employed. This strategy will include

_____
(types of promotion)

Distribution of the product or service will be achieved by _____.

A _____ pricing strategy will be used. This was decided because
(penetration/skimming)

_____

_____.

Competition: The strengths of the competition data will be overcome by..........WHO ARE

YOUR MAJOR COMPETITORS?   WHAT SHARE OF THE MARKET DO THEY

PRESENTLY HAVE?   WHAT ARE THEIR STRENGTHS AND WEAKNESSES?   HOW

WILL YOU OVERCOME THEIR STRENGTHS AND OBTAIN A VIABLE SHARE OF THE

MARKET? WHAT SHARE OF THE MARKET DO YOU HOPE TO OBTAIN AND WHEN?

Research indicated that there are _____ major immediate competitors.
(# of competitors)

The major competitors are: _____,

_____, _____,

_____ and _____.

They have _____, _____, _____ and _____ percent shares of the market respectively.

COMPETITOR ANALYSIS

Competitor Name	Strengths	Weaknesses

Personnel: Discuss all of your personnel requirements. Discuss all of the activities that will be necessary in order for your firm to accomplish its objectives, and then discuss the type of people you plan to hire to complete these activities. Make sure to address qualifications, compensation plans, and any other major personnel considerations. Discuss the <u>key management personnel</u>, with particular attention being paid to their experience in the industry and their qualifications. Attach resumes for all key personnel. Devote a separate section to addressing the qualifications of the business owner. Don't fail to include a narrative about your success qualities which were discussed and assessed earlier in this manual.

Initially, _____ will have _____.
                        (name of business)   (# employees)

They will hold the following positions and have the following responsibilities:

Positions	Responsibilities

Personnel will be compensated based on _____.

Key Personnel: The key personnel are (include yourself):

Their qualifications and functions are as follows:

Position	Qualifications	Functions

Organizational Structure: After you have determined the types of activities necessary to fulfill your organization's objectives, you can determine the most logical way for these activities to interact within the confines of the organization. Who does what? Who is accountable to whom? Diagram your organizational structure. Initially, the organizational structure may only consist of you, but think about growth planning.

Production: Describe the facilities necessary to house the operations of your business. Discuss any lease or purchase arrangements and all facility-improvement plans along with costs for these arrangements and plans. Re-examine the rationale for your selection of the facility and the lease or purchase decision.

If you are producing a product or service, discuss production in detail. Address inventory and quality control considerations as well as costs.

Facilities

Initially, _____ will be housed in _____.
(name of business)   (describe facility)

The facility consists of. . . . .

Equipment

Explain in detail and list all required equipment, fixtures, etc. Assess the costs and discuss the purchase and lease arrangements and payment terms.

Supplies

List all of your supply requirements including the names of the suppliers and the terms of payment. Assess the reasoning behind the selection of a supplier. Include delivery time, order quantities and backup sources for all supplies. (See Chapter XII.)

Insurance

List insurance coverage to be carried on your business facility, equipment, officers and liability coverage.

Accounting Firm

Discuss your selection of an accounting firm, the services they will be performing and the costs for these services. Include the address of the accounting firm.

The business will use the accounting services of _____.
(name of accounting firm)

Their services have been obtained because _____.

They will provide the following services _____.

Banks/Financial Institutions

_____

_____

_____

Legal Counsel

Discuss services to be performed and costs.

_____

_____

_____

Critical Risks and Problems

_____

_____

_____

Growth Plans

_____

_____

_____

Financial Information

The next step is to translate your business plan into dollars. Make sure to include profit/loss forecasts, pro forma balance sheets, cash flow projections, and break-even analysis.

Make sure that you have inserted all of the pertinent cost information on your cost sheets and that you have transferred them to the appropriate financial statements. Thoroughly assess your capital requirements necessary to get your business off the ground and running for at least one year.

Appendix

Provide Support Documentation (Including, but not limited to, the following:

- Resumes of Key Personnel

- Personal Financial Statements

- Credit Reports

- Letters of Reference

- Copies of Leases (if applicable)

- Contracts (if applicable)

- Legal Documents

- Insurance Policies

- Partnership Agreements or Corporation Charter (if applicable)

- Patents

- Copyrights

- Trademarks

- Buy/Sell Contract

- Promotional Material

- Photographs (if deemed appropriate)

- Brochures (or other promotional documents)

"There are few joys greater in life than living your dreams and seeing your business idea turn into a business reality."

M.G.L.J.

CHAPTER IV

Marketing

"The entrepreneur is a walking and talking billboard

for her business. You must present a professional

appearance at all times, even in the grocery store."

M.G.L.J.

MARKETING

Regardless of the type of business one selects to start, there will be a product or service that needs to be sold or marketed to the public. Contrary to old beliefs of production orientation where firms decided what they wanted to make and then attempted to sell the product, it is advisable for firms to adhere to the marketing-orientation concept. This concept holds that firms should seek to satisfy their customers at a profit. This involves determining the needs and wants of a selected customer group first, and then attempting to satisfy their desires. Encompassed here is the selection of a **target market**, a group of individuals to whom you want to direct your efforts and attempt to satisfy, followed by the manipulation of what is called the **marketing mix** to satisfy this target market. The **marketing mix** (or the 4 P's), include the **product, price, place,** and **promotion**. In other words, you must come up with the right product, at the right price, at the right place and use the right promotion to satisfy the chosen target market. The "four P's" are explained in the following sections.

Product

The product component of the marketing mix includes not only the specific good or service offered for sale, but also its reputation, name, packaging, image, as well as the accompanying services and innovative services, such as incorporating foreign language into the learning program. The product of a flower business, in fact, does not have to be physical at all but could be the rendering of related services such as delivery and floral design consultation for funerals and weddings.

The beauty of the product is also an important component of a marketing strategy. The visual appeal of your product will bring you additional customers when others marvel at your floral designs, the uniqueness of your gifts, and your overall presentation of the product. Potential customers will ask, "What florist designed that beautiful arrangement?" The answer will stay in the potential customer's mind until they need the services of a florist or a special, unique gift item.

Therefore, the total product offered by a firm may include a large array of goods as well as related services such as parking facilities and credit. Total product planning is obviously crucial in order to provide the "right" product for the selected target market. Total product planning needs to encompass cognition of **product life cycles**. Like humans, products go through life cycles. The **life cycle** of products is generally divided into several stages: **product introduction, market growth, market maturity, sales decline,** and **termination**.

The **introduction stage** involves informing the target market of the existence of the product or service as well as its advantages and uses. During the introductory stage, a great deal of money is spent on promoting the product. The business may experience losses since money is invested in the business at this point for future benefits.

During the **growth stage**, the business owner will begin to make a profit. As other firms or individuals see the entrepreneur making money, others will try to imitate the product. Competition, therefore, becomes strong during this phase.

During the **market maturity stage**, many competitors have entered the market. Competition may be very fierce and could cause profits to decline. Advertising, thus, becomes very important. This phase, as well as the other stages, could last for any period of time.

During the **sales decline phase**, new products begin to replace the old. If a firm sees its "total" product moving into the sales decline phase, intense planning needs to be conducted to alter the product or even change products or the nature of the business before sales decline significantly. However, product planning needs to be conducted continuously so as to avoid getting into the sales-decline predicament. Entrepreneurs must be ever conscious of their environment to be prepared to change direction or alter strategies and/or products quickly.

The **termination phase** involves the termination of product sales because a market no longer exists for the product, or the product is obsolete because of new technological advances or alternative choices formerly not available.

Surveying the Market for Product Marketability

You need to see if your perception of the need for your product or service is the same as your identified customer group, or target market, which you wish to serve. At this point, an interview of constituents in your target market should be conducted to see if your identified customer group desires your product or service, or whether your business idea is satisfying any need except your need to be in business for yourself.

A brief questionnaire should be drawn up and presented either verbally or in written form. Questions should be designed to give you specific answers, but at the same time open enough for respondents to possibly give you some ideas for product or service changes when they respond. The sample questionnaire which follows should serve as a guide in designing a survey for your business idea. Be sure to survey as many individuals as possible who are in your target market.

Sample Questionnaire

We are conducting a survey to determine the desire for fresh flowers, plants, and gift items in the Atlanta area. Please be kind enough to answer the following brief questions.

1. **From which stores do you presently purchase your fresh flowers and gift plants?**
   (Check all that apply)
   - Supermarket
   - Superstore (i.e., WalMart)
   - Convenience market
   - Flower shop (please indicate shop you frequent and its location)_____
   - Other_____

2. **Were you satisfied with your purchases? (Yes/No)_____. If you were not satisfied, what displeased you?**_____

3. **What features would make a flower shop offering floral arrangements, gift plants, and related gift items attractive to you?**
   (Check all that apply)

o Selection	o Delivery service
o Quality	o Internet services and sales availability
o Uniqueness of floral design and items offered	o FTD or other wire service
o Convenience to work	o Gift wrapping
o Convenience to home	o Gift reminder service (store contacts you about an upcoming birthday, anniversary or special annual occasion).
o Cost	
o Dependability or reliability	
o Past positive experience	o Other_____
o Personal service and attention	

4. **In what types of flowers and gifts are you generally interested ?**
   (Check all that apply)

o Green Plants	o Juice baskets
o Dish gardens	o Brass gift items
o Tree-type plants	o Oriental gift items
o Silk arrangements	o Porcelain/crystal gift items
o Fresh bouquets	o Silver gift items
o Fruit baskets	o Other _____
o Balloons	

5. **For which occasions are you most likely to purchase flowers, plants, or gifts?**

(Check all that apply)

o Birthday	o Love and Romance
o Get Well	o Thank You
o Mother's Day	o Thinking of You
o Father's Day	o Congratulations
o Sympathy	o Flowers or Plants for Your Home
o Wedding	o Other _____
o Corporate Gifts	

6. **In what price range do you expect to pay for a floral gift or a get well wish?**

o $25 - 44 _____	o $65 - 84 _____
o $45 - 64 _____	o $85 or above _____

7. **Please provide the following information about yourself.**

Sex ____M ____F	**Ethnic Background** _____
Married ____ **Single** ____	**Occupation** _____
Household income range:	**Rent** _____ **Own Home** _____
under $40,000 _____	
	Section of city where you reside:
$40,001-60,000 _____	
$60,001-80,000 _____	_____
	Section of city where you do most of your floral shopping:
$80,001-90,000 _____	
above $90,000 _____	_____

8. **Would you patronize a floral and gift shop located at_____?**
   (Insert where you are thinking about locating.)

Thank you so very much for your time and your responses.

Evaluate your questionnaire responses. Does the result of the questionnaire information indicate that your target market desires the service you offer? Does your target market need to be changed or widened? Does your total service/product need changing?

It must now be determined whether the service offered is technically feasible, whether it could achieve a competitive advantage, and if the cost and time necessary for development are worthwhile.

A. <u>Status</u>

1. What is the current stage of development of the venture's service (introduction, maturity, etc.)? Is there something that gives your service a "new twist" in the minds of the public?

If the service needs licenses, indicate which ones and all the procedures necessary for obtaining them. Also indicate all permits or certificates as applicable.

2. What must be done to get the service ready for sale? Think in terms of the total product and packaging.

B. Strengths and Weaknesses

Strengths

      1. Indicate any patents, trademarks or trade secrets on your service. Do these give

      you a competitive advantage?

      2. What design features of your service give it an advantage over the

      competition?

      3. What is your estimate of the life expectancy of your service?

Weaknesses

    1. Are there any features of your service that may put it at a disadvantage in the

    marketplace?

    2. Indicate any possibilities of rapid change in demand because of population trends

    and/or developments such as an increased number of new competitors among grocery

    stores.

Price

Price is another one of the "four P's" which the entrepreneur can adjust to satisfy the

target market. A pricing strategy must be developed. The entrepreneur must determine whether

products generally will be priced higher, lower, or the same as the competition. Initially, the products could be offered at a price lower than the competition's to obtain a high sales volume, with prices raised later **(penetration pricing)**; or the products could be offered initially at a high price and lowered later **(skimming pricing)**. The entrepreneur also has the task of determining the specific price of all products and/or services. With pricing the product or service, there are many factors to consider. Included are: channel of distribution used, competition's pricing strategy, annual anticipated sales volume, product life cycle, opportunity for special promotions, the image of the product, and operation expenses.

Place

A major part of place considerations is the determination of the appropriate channel of distribution to use for the product to get to the target market. There are four basic channels of distribution that the entrepreneur may want to consider, and of course, there are many variations of the four.

BASIC CHANNELS OF DISTRIBUTION

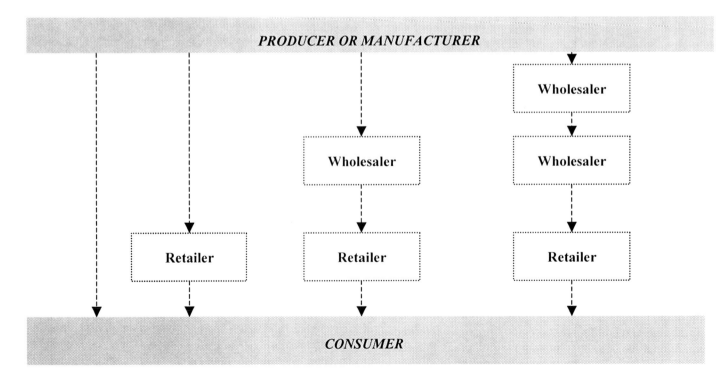

Promotion

Promotion involves persuading the target market to purchase your product or service. Sales promotion can use either direct or indirect methods. **Direct** promotion methods include advertising, publicity, displays, special event sales, and personal selling; whereas, **indirect** promotion methods include public relations, customer relations, customer services, and product packaging. Another part of promotion is advertising. For the new firm, advertising is particularly important because new or potential customers must be made aware of the firm's existence. Even though word-of-mouth advertising is fine and, in fact, crucial, a firm cannot rely solely on this form of advertising. Small business people need to incorporate advertising costs into their budgets, allocating monthly amounts in this area. To be successful, advertising must be consistent, image building, and continuous. The new entrepreneur needs to start off with advertising which will bring immediate action (i.e., immediate response ads).

There are a variety of advertising media which can be used.

- Newspapers

- Magazines

- Radio

- Direct Mail

- Television

- Web Sites

- Point-of-Purchase Displays

- Bench Advertising

- Billboards

- Motion Advertising (public transportation)

- Fliers and Brochures

- Speciality Items or Novelty Items (such as pens, calendars, etc.)

- Free Publicity

- Telephone Yellow Pages

The selection of the best media for a small firm is not an easy endeavor. Television is not appropriate for most small firms due to the cost factor and the probability that you may be reaching many individuals who are not in your target market, thus incurring unnecessary costs. Large newspapers also tend to be quite expensive. Local or community papers also tend to be somewhat expensive; however, local or community papers may be a viable option. Magazines also tend to be costly; and with the exception of local magazines, may cover too much territory for a small business. Advertising spots on a local radio station may be feasible if the costs are in line and you can get the most advantageous time for reaching your target market.

Billboards often are effective near the location of the business but also are costly. Speciality advertisement, which includes calendars, rain scarves, and pens, tends to be effective and can be as costly or as inexpensive as you desire. Motion advertising tends to be effective if your market uses transportation such as buses, taxis, and subways on a routine basis. The use of the telephone book should not be overlooked, as many potential customers do pre-shopping by the phone. Direct-mail advertising is used by a great number of small businesses. It is less expensive than many other forms of advertising and provides the small business owner with selective coverage. Your floral business should consider having a Web site which would detail all of your products and services. A Web site is really a "must have" in the 21st Century.

The goal of advertising is to sell by way of the **"AIDA"** formula. This formula means you must get the potential customers' **<u>attention,</u>** make them **<u>interested</u>** in your product or service, create a **<u>desire</u>** for your product, and bring about **<u>action</u>**--the purchase of your product or service.

Basic Advertising Guidelines

1. **Start with the sales budget.**

   - Decide what percentage of your anticipated sales volume you will allocate to advertising. Use the following approach: research trade journals, estimate monthly sales, and consider special promotions.

2. **Profile yourself and your customers.**

   - What business am I in?

   - What quality of products do I sell?

   - What kind of image do I want to project?

   - How do I compare with the competition?

   - What customer services do I offer?

   - What are my customers' tastes?

   - Why will they buy from me?

3. **Select the appropriate advertising media for your business.**

4. **Adhere to the following pointers for printed ads.**

   - Make ads easy to recognize.

   - Use simple layouts.

   - Use dominant illustrations to feature services.

   - Show the product's benefits to the reader.

   - State a price or range of prices.

   - Include the business name, address, phone number, e-mail address, and Web site.

- Repeat an ad if the response is good.

5. AIDA: Get the customers' **attention,** arouse their **interest**, make them **desire** your product and finally, get them to take **action** or buy your product. This is the goal of advertising.

Measuring the Results of Advertising

There are different types of advertisements and different measuring methods. **Immediate-response** advertising is designed to cause the potential customer to buy a particular product from you within a short time. The following is a list of tests to measure the response to the advertisements.

- Coupons brought in,
- Requests by phone or letters referring to the ad,
- Sales made of a particular service, and
- Business traffic

Attitude advertising is the reputation or image builder form of advertising. To measure its effectiveness:

- Run an ad every week and compare each week's sales with the same week of the previous year, and
- Ask customers how they heard about your business

Make sure your marketing strategy includes a focus on buyer influencers, such as wedding consultants and funeral homes.

Wedding consultants often direct brides and grooms to flower shops for arrangement designs and bouquets to make that special day memorable. That also brings to light those complementary items that may be desired by a bride and groom, such as flower preservation of the bride's bouquet and gifts for the bridal family.

When families are at a time of grief, they often rely on the funeral home for advice on everything; and that includes referrals to good florists. Even friends of the family or the deceased will call the funeral home for a referral to a reputable florist or to the florist the family is using. Many sending sympathy flowers are also often in search of a unique sympathy gift that may include flowers or plants, but also something memorable that the loved ones of the deceased can keep for a long period of time. This opens the market for sympathy gift items, such as sympathy gift baskets with a religious theme including angels, picture frames and albums for family members to place their cherished special pictures of the deceased, bibles and appropriate religious books with words of comfort. Sympathy gift baskets can also include items for tranquillity and relaxation, such as soothing teas with teapots, special bath fragrances, and potpourri. The possibilities and opportunities are endless.

Marketing Research

Marketing research is essentially a systematic way of finding general information that pertains to the marketing of one's own goods or services or learning about one's customers and/or competition. It assists one in determining who should be in the target market (group of people to whom you are addressing your efforts and trying to satisfy) and the demographic information and spending habits of those potential customers. In addition, it helps to verify whether you have the goods and/or services the customers want and whether the promotional strategy is appropriate and effective.

There are two major types of marketing research: **secondary** and **primary**. **Secondary** involves the utilization of published information, such as surveys, books, and magazines. **Primary** research pertains to information obtained directly from one's target market. Primary research may take the form of a questionnaire (direct mail or personal), telephone surveys, test marketing, behavior observation, etc.

Marketing research does not have to be expensive because a great amount of the information can be gathered by the entrepreneur. License plates of cars in the parking area or neighborhood can provide an idea of where customers or potential customers live (county) so that advertising can be directed accordingly. Also, questionnaires can be utilized; and the examination of telephone numbers given on a mailing list or personal check can provide an idea of the section of the city in which customers live. Coupons used in connection with radio ads that require customers to mention a radio station's name to get a special discount will also help to determine who is hearing certain ads. Of course, an observant entrepreneur is necessary.

Looking at how customers dress, whether they are married and/or have children, and what age, ethnic background, likes, dislikes, and what other characteristics they possess is also important.

Using some form of marketing research, the potential entrepreneur needs to estimate the approximate size of the total potential market.

Attempt to estimate your market size. Indicate sources of data for your approximation. Some of the references from the bibliography should be helpful here. The approximate size of my market is _____.

It is also necessary to thoroughly analyze your competition. A table such as the one that follows may be helpful with this endeavor.

ANAYLSIS OF COMPETITION

Name and Address of Competitor	% Estimated Market Share	Estimated Yearly Sales $	Comments on Competitor's Strengths and Weaknesses

How can you overcome your competitors' strengths to gain a competitive edge?

What market share (% of the market) do you think you can acquire?

Marketing Tactics

1. What methods will you use to sell your service (direct selling, Web site, yellow pages, radio ads, etc.)?

2. What are your marketing strategies?

3. Will you offer unique services and/or specialized care services?

4. How will you bring your service to the attention of potential customers?

5. What type of advertising will you use?

6. How much will it cost and how long will it take to establish a market share for your service? (Make a rough estimate.)

Examining the Economic Environment of Your Business

The total environment in which your business will be operating must also be considered when determining an appropriate marketing strategy. The North American Industry Classification System (NAICS) Code for flower shops offering fresh flowers is 453110 (former Standard Industrial Classification (SIC) code: 5992). This industry consists of establishments known as florists primarily engaged in retailing cut flowers, floral arrangements, and potted plants purchased from others. These establishments usually prepare the arrangements they sell. The U.S. Census Bureau NAICS Code for flower shops, artificial or dried, is 453998 (former SIC Code: 5999).

The U.S. Census Bureau NAICS Code for gift shops is 453220 (former SIC Code: 5947). This industry comprises establishments primarily engaged in retailing new gifts, novelty merchandise, souvenirs, greeting cards, seasonal and holiday decorations, and curios.

The following questions should be addressed.

1. How many firms are in this industry?

2. Do they vary in size?

3. Where are most of the enterprises located?

4. What is the relationship between small firms of this type and larger firms in the industry?

5. Do the firms serve English-speaking only or some bilingual markets?

6. What is the government's attitude toward this type of business?

7. What is society's attitude about your type of business or your industry?

8. What is the market for your business? Consider age, sex, education, birth rate, population trends, income, competition, etc. of your target market.

*"To be a successful entrepreneur, you must be **results-oriented** and **resilient** with a keen understanding of the importance of **relationships** and **respect**."*

M.G.L.J.

CHAPTER V

Forms of Business Ownership

" *Look into the future with vision and vivaciously*

create a business climate based on values. "

M.G.L.J.

FORMS OF BUSINESS OWNERSHIP

There are three major legal forms of business ownership: the **sole proprietorship**, **partnership,** and **corporation**. One form cannot be said to be better than the other, as one must consider the advantages and disadvantages of each in light of his or her needs and desires. Below, the three forms are evaluated in terms of their advantages and disadvantages.

Proprietorship

An enterprise owned by one individual is a **proprietorship**. The owner and the business are one and the same and cannot be legally distinguished and separated in the eyes of the law. This is the most common form of legal ownership.

Advantages

- It is fairly easy to start.

- Legal assistance is not a necessity.

- The organizational structure is simple.

- The owner has freedom to make decisions and enjoy the profits.

- It is easy to dissolve.

- The owner is liable for all the enterprise's debts.

- Liability is not limited to the amount of capital/total assets invested in the business. The owner's home, car, bank account, and other possessions may be claimed by people to whom he or she owes money.

- If the owner has personal debts, creditors can take assets of the business to satisfy demands.

- Sometimes it is difficult to obtain funding.

- Success is dependent on the owner's abilities.

- The legal life of the business terminates with the death of the owner.

Partnership

A **partnership** is the joining of two or more individuals to form an organization.

Advantages

- Gives you the opportunity to pool financial resources together.

- Provides the advantages of combining the additional skills and knowledge of partners. Allows the teaming of individuals who have complementary talent.

- Allows for division of labor and management responsibility.

Disadvantages

- General partners have unlimited liability.

- The death of a partner terminates the partnership.

- General partners are responsible for the acts of each other partner.

- Partners cannot obtain bonding protection against the acts of other partners.

- There is the possibility of disagreement among partners.

There are two different types of partnerships:

1) **General** - Each partner is held liable for the acts of other partners.

2) **Limited** - This form can only be created by compliance with a state's statutory requirements. It is composed of one or more general partners. The liability of the limited partner is limited to the amount of funds he or she contributes.

A partnership should have an attorney draw up a partnership agreement. The partnership agreement usually includes sections addressing the following:

- name, purpose, and location

- duration of agreement

- type of partnership

- contribution by partners

- business expansion (how it will be handled)

- authority

- books, records, and the method of accounting

- division of profits and losses

- salaries

- rights of continuing partnership

- death of partner

- employee negotiations

- release of debts

- sale of partnership interests

- arbitration

- addition, alterations, and/or modification of partnership agreement

- settlement of disputes

- required and prohibited acts

- absence and disability

Corporation

A **corporation** is a legal entity which is separate and distinct from the individual. In the new or very small corporation, the stock in the corporation is described as "closed" or "closely held" and is not available to the general public in order for the owners to keep control.

Advantages

- The corporate form of ownership offers permanence--the business does not cease to exist if an owner dies.

- Owners of a corporation have limited liability (only the amount invested in the business).

- Corporations usually have greater borrowing power.

- Transferring ownership is relatively easy.

- Company expansion is relatively easy.

- In figuring the corporation's net income, salaries paid to employees and executives may be deducted as an expense item.

Disadvantages

- Incorporations can be costly and require detailed records which are often costly and time consuming.

- Corporate income is taxed twice. First, the corporation pays tax on its income before it distributes dividends, and then shareholders pay taxes on dividends.

- The powers of the corporation are limited to those stated in the charter.

- The corporate form of ownership is more impersonal than the other forms.

S Corporations

The **S Corporation**, formerly known as the Subchapter S Corporation, is a form of organization which is specifically designed for closely held firms. The major difference between this type of corporation and regular corporations is the way in which they are taxed. In S Corporations, the profits are distributed to shareholders according to how much stock they own. The shareholders pay tax on the profits as personal income, with the corporation paying no tax as an entity. In essence, the stockholders are taxed as partners, thus avoiding the corporate income tax structure while allowing the firm to retain the limited liability feature of corporations.

S Corporations have many legal restrictions, including limitations to the number of stockholders, who may be stockholders, how profits are distributed, and the amount of fringe benefits allowed owner/employees.

You should consult your attorney and accountant to determine the advantages and disadvantages of this and other forms of ownership for your particular business. You should also consult your accountant about all tax considerations prior to actually implementing your business.

Limited Liability Company

The **Limited Liability Company (LLC)** is a hybrid between a partnership and a corporation in that it combines the "pass-through" treatment of a partnership with the limited liability accorded to corporate shareholders.

Advantages

- Historically, most states require that a Limited Liability Corporation (LLC) be comprised of at least two LLC members. Today, most states and the IRS recognize the single-member LLC as a legitimate business structure.

- Like limited partnerships and corporations, the Limited Liability Corporation shares a similar advantage--it is recognized as a separate legal entity from its "members."

- Most states require fewer formalities be observed in an LLC in comparison to a corporation.

- The LLC owner's liability is generally limited to the amount of money which the person has invested in the LLC. Thus, LLC members are offered the same limited liability protection as a corporation's shareholders.

- LLCs allow for pass-through taxation. This means that earnings of an LLC are taxed only once. The earnings of an LLC are treated like the earnings from a partnership, sole proprietorships, and most S corporations.

- Like general partnerships, LLCs are usually free to establish any organizational structure agreed on by the members. Thus, profit interests may be separated from voting interests.

Disadvantages

* Some states require that a LLC have more than one member

* Legal assistance is required to set up

* More paperwork is necessary than for an ordinary partnership

* Some states require that a dissolution date be listed in the articles of organization. This date may be amended. Further, certain events, such as death of a member, a member leaving, bankruptcy, etc. can be a dissolution event. A corporation has unlimited life, and these events are not dissolution events for a corporation.

* The LLC is a newer entity, and people are not as familiar with the LLC as a corporation.

The major legal considerations for a small business are as follows:

I. Choice of organizational form of ownership

   A. Proprietorship
   B. Partnership (general or limited)
   C. Corporation

II. Issues to address in organizational documents

   A. Procedures for voting
   B. Admission of new parties
   C. Providing continuity
   D. Resolving deadlocks
   E. Continuity in the event of death, disability, or bankruptcy of an owner
   F. Sources of capital

III. Business issues to consider in structuring a company

   A. Exposure to liability

      1. Product liability
      2. Environmental protection
      3. Errors and omissions

4. Fraud allegations
5. Worker compensation
6. Defamation
7. Trademark and copyright infringement

B. Regulatory authorities

1. Licenses and permits
2. Securities regulation
3. Consumer protection
4. Labor relations
5. Environmental protection

IV. Registration with taxing authorities

A. Federal income taxes
B. Federal employment taxes and withholding
C. State employment taxes
D. Federal excise taxes
E. State sales and use taxes
F. State franchise and excise taxes
G. Miscellaneous state taxes
H. Local general property tax

Franchising

Franchising is a form of licensing by which the owner of a product, service, or process obtains distribution at the retail level through affiliated dealers. The owner of the product or service is called the **franchisor**. The affiliated dealer is known as the **franchisee**. Common franchises include McDonalds, Burger King, and Kiddie Academy. Franchising is an option with many benefits. The benefits, however, vary from company to company.

Benefits

1. Franchising provides a chance to open a business without previous experience.

2. Franchising often provides a chance to open a business with less capital.

3. Many franchises provide financial assistance.

4. Franchises generally have a consumer-accepted image.

5. Franchises offer consistent quality.

6. Franchising affords combined buying power, allowing for purchasing advantages.

7. Franchises offer basic training and continued assistance.

8. Franchises provide location analysis.

9. Franchising provides the financial capability to buy a choice location.

10. Franchising provides advantageous rental or leasing rates.

11. Franchisers assist in the development of well-designed facilities, fixtures and displays, and provide supplies.

12. Franchisers offer managerial and records assistance.

13. Franchisers offer sales, advertising, and marketing assistance.

14. Franchisers provide national publicity, promotion, and recognition.

15. Franchising affords higher income potential.

16. Franchises have a lower rate of failure.

17. Franchises provide continual research and development.

Disadvantages

Some of the disadvantages of franchising includes:

1. The subjugation of personal identity.

2. The submission to significant standardization and control.

3. The franchisee does not have the option of selecting unique services to offer.

Pointers for Evaluating a Franchise Opportunity

Before going into any franchise arrangement, the opportunity needs to be evaluated thoroughly. The following steps should be used when evaluating an opportunity:

- Check the opportunity out with the Better Business Bureau and Chamber of Commerce.

- Determine when the business was established.

- Determine what type of financing is provided.

- Ask the owners for a sample contract and study it with the advice of legal counsel.

- Determine if the company provides continual assistance.

- Find out how many of the franchises are now operating and where they are located.

- Determine what the failure rate for the franchises has been.

- Investigate how profits are running.

- Research the product's or service's quality.

- Evaluate the contract to be sure it covers all aspects of the agreement.

- Investigate what types of promotion will be provided.

Franchising Checklist

Before any franchise agreement is signed, determine whether enough information about the proposed relationship has been obtained to understand fully the implications of the agreement. The following checklist may be useful in making that determination.[18]

The Company

How long has the firm been in business?
Has it a reputation for honesty and fair dealing?
How does it rate with the Better Business Bureau?
Is the firm adequately financed so that it can carry out its stated plan of financial assistance and expansion?
Has the franchisor shown you any certified figures indicating exact net profits of one or more operating firms which you have checked personally?
How selective is it in choosing franchisees?
Has the franchisor investigated you carefully enough to assure itself that you can successfully operate one of its franchises?

The Product

What is the product's quality?
How well is it selling?
Have you conducted a study to determine whether the product or service which you propose to sell has a market in your territory at   the prices you will have to charge?
Is the product priced competitively?
Is it packaged attractively?
How long has it been on the market?
Where else is it sold?
Will the product or service you are considering be in greater demand, about the same, or less demand five years from now?

The Sales Area

Is the territory well defined?
Is it large enough to offer good sales potential?
What are its growth possibilities?

Does the franchise give you exclusive territorial rights or can the franchisor sell a second or third franchise in your territory?

Is the franchisor connected in any way with any other franchise company offering similar merchandise or services?

If the answer is yes, what is your protection against this second franchisor organization?

What competition exists in your territory for the product or service you contemplate selling?

What is the territory's income level? Are there fluctuations in income?

Will the population in the territory increase, remain static, or decrease over the next five years?

The Contract

Does the contract cover all aspects of the agreement?

Does it benefit both parties?

Has your lawyer approved the franchise contract?

Does the franchise call upon you to take any steps which are, according to your lawyer, unwise or illegal in your state, county, or city?

Can the contract be renewed, terminated, or transferred?

Under what conditions will the franchise be lost?

What are the conditions for obtaining a license?

Under what circumstances and at what cost can you terminate the franchise contract?

If you sell your franchise, will you be compensated for your goodwill; or will the goodwill you have built into the business be lost by you?

Is a certain size and type of operation specified?

Is there an additional fixed payment each year?

Is there a percent of gross sales payment?

Must a certain amount of merchandise be purchased?

Is there an annual sales quota?

Can the franchisee return merchandise for credit?

Can the franchisee engage in other business activities?

Does the franchisor provide continuing assistance?

Will the firm assist you in finding a good location?

Is there training for franchisees and key employees?

Are manuals, sales kits, and/or accounting systems supplied?

Does the franchisor handle lease arrangements?

Does he or she design the store layout and displays?

Does he or she select opening inventory?

Does he or she provide inventory control methods?

Does he or she provide market surveys?

Does he or she help finance equipment?

Does he or she make direct loans to qualified individuals?

Does he or she actively promote the product or service?

How and where is the product being advertised?
What advertising aid does the franchisor provide?
What is the franchisee's share of advertising costs?
Exactly what can the franchisor do for you that you cannot do for yourself?

Questions Pertaining to Ownership

Answer the following questions to assess some of the key aspects of deciding what form of business organization is best for your firm.

What legal structure would insure the greatest adaptability for the administration of your firm?

What are the possibilities of attracting additional capital?

What are the needs for and possibilities of attracting additional expertise?

Which legal structure would best serve your purpose? Why?

"Formula for perpetual ignorance: Think you know it all."

M.G.L.J.

CHAPTER VI

Taking Over An Established Business

" Successful entrepreneurs are intuitive, display

integrity in all of their actions, and approach

challenging situations with ingenuity."

M.G.L.J.

NEW BUSINESS VERSUS AN ESTABLISHED BUSINESS

The question may have already crossed your mind as to whether to buy a business that is already operating or to begin your own. Below are some considerations you should address when evaluating this question.

Just because a business is already established does not mean that success is guaranteed. The same very careful analysis that is conducted for a new enterprise must be done for an established business, including the consideration of target markets, location factors, and capital requirements.

Acquiring an Established Business

Both pros and cons must be considered when the entrepreneur is making the decision about the feasibility of acquiring an existing enterprise.

The Pros

1. The building, equipment and people are already functioning.

2. The product is already being produced.

3. A market is established for the product or service.

4. Revenue is probably being generated.

5. The location may be desirable.

6. Financial relationships have been established.

7. Inventory is already in place.

8. Verifiable information about the business and industry can be obtained from the previous owner.

The Cons

1. The facilities may be old.

2. The personnel may be poor and inappropriate for the new owner.

3. Union/management relations may be bad.

4. The inventory, if any, may be out-of-date and useless.

5. The location may be poor.

6. The financial condition may be poor.

7. The firm's bad reputation may be inherited.

8. Space may be too expensive.

9. Equipment may be obsolete.

10. You may not know the real reason why the previous owner is giving up the business.

11. Records may be misleading.

When taking over an established business, there are six factors which should be closely examined.

- The real reason why the business is being terminated.

- The company's past sales and profits.

- The operating costs of the business (the use of operating ratios can be quite beneficial here).

- The condition of equipment and inventory (Is it old, obsolete, and/or in need of repair?).

- The value and condition of tangible assets.

- The value of the business as compared to the price being asked.

How to Enter an Existing Business

Examine the condition of the business by addressing the following:

1. Are the physical facilities run down?

2. Does the inventory contain mostly dead stock?

3. Is the market for the firm's product declining?

4. Is the business solvent?

5. What are the intentions of the present owner (e.g.,health, retirement, or competition)?

Business Evaluation Pointers

Useful ways of analyzing an existing enterprise include the following options.

- Analyze accounting information, and do a physical inventory to determine the accuracy of recorded data.

- Determine whether the firm's cash position is high or low compared to the industry.

- Use financial ratios to determine the health of the firm. The following ratios are commonly used in the examination of the health of a firm.

Current Ratio: Current Assets
                    Current Liabilities

MEASURES SHORT-TERM SOLVENCY. SHOULD BE AROUND 2/1.

Quick Ratio: Current Assets - Inventory
                 Current Liabilities

SHOWS ABILITY TO PAY SHORT-TERM OBLIGATIONS WITHOUT HAVING TO SELL INVENTORY.

Debt to Equity Ratio: <u>Current Liabilities + Long-term Liabilities</u>
Equity
Note: Owner's Equity = Assets - Liabilities

SHOWS FIRM'S OBLIGATIONS TO CREDITORS

- Determine the amount of debt and the terms of that debt.

- Determine the validity of the financial statements.

- Check the age of the accounts receivable.

- Check the cash flow.

- Appraise the pricing formula.

- Appraise operations, plant, and equipment.

- How effective are personnel?

- What is the quality of production?

- What is the physical condition of the plant? Is the layout appropriate for your needs?

- What are the age and condition of the equipment?

- Conduct a feasibility study.

Establishing a New Business

So, why start a business from the ground up? Consider the pros and cons.

The Pros

1. You can create the physical facilities you want.

2. All modern equipment can be utilized as opposed to inheriting outdated equipment, as may be the case when taking over an established business.

3. Modern processes and procedures can be implemented.

4. New inventory can be purchased.

5. New personnel can be hired.

6. You can design your own management system.

The Cons

1. There may be a problem of selecting the right business to start.

2. The business has unproven performance records in sales, reliability, service, and profits.

3. There are problems in finding a location, building, equipment, and personnel.

4. The owner must train a new work force.

5. There is no established service quality.

6. There will be problems at the start.

7. There may be problems with establishing an appropriate accounting system.

8. There will initially be "bugs" in the operations.

9. There may be problems with establishing a customer or client base.

"Your reputation is your most valuable asset."

M.G.L.J.

CHAPTER VII

Location

"Be deliberate in your actions and move with

determination and dignity."

M.G.L.J.

LOCATION

The importance of a good location should not be overlooked. Frequently, a prospective entrepreneur in search of a business home will take a location simply because a vacancy exists. Many factors need to be considered when examining a possible location.

Reaching Potential Customers

An overall assessment should be made of the city or town in which one wishes to locate to determine its receptiveness to her or his type of business. More specifically, one should examine the territory where he or she expects to find customers and determine if the specific site will serve the needs of the potential customers. The following questions should be considered:

1. Do the identified potential customers have the money to afford the services you will be offering?

2. What are the neighborhood service-use patterns?

3. Is transportation convenient to the business?

4. What are the traffic patterns and volume near the proposed business location?

5. Is there a good primary and secondary road access to the business?

6. Are there plans for new road construction or alteration of the present roads which may involve the disruption of traffic near the business and/or a by-pass of the area?

7. Is there a good pool of qualified personnel available in the area?

Consider the enterprise location's proximity to major employers, public transportation, traffic arteries, etc. Further considerations are air quality and other environmental factors that impact outdoor activities (e.g., traffic, noise and volume, street safety, etc.).

Another factor to consider in site location is the proximity of competition. It is necessary to investigate the number of similar establishments competing for the same target market. Parking is a matter also deserving consideration. Ample parking is crucial in any business whose customers visit the business via car.

Of course, selecting a suitable building is also necessary; but this goes without saying and rests on good judgment as to the appropriateness of the facilities for the needs of the business.

LOCATION CONSIDERATIONS

Grade each factor: "E" for excellent, "G" for good, "F" for fair, and "P" for poor.

Factor	Grade
Centrally located to reach your target market	
Supplies and equipment readily available	
Nearby competition situation	
Transportation availability and rates	
Quantity and quality of available employees	
Prevailing rates of employee pay	
Parking facilities	
Adequacy of utilities (sewer, water, power, gas)	
Traffic flow	
Tax burden	
Crime/Safety factors	
Quality of police and fire protection	
Physical suitability of building	
Type and cost of lease or mortgage	
Provision for future expansion	
Other businesses promoting area	
Image of area as it relates to business image	
Zoning restrictions	

"You can always tell the pioneers by the number of arrows in

their backs. "

M.G.L.J.

CHAPTER VIII

Staffing

"It's very difficult to find good, capable, dependable, honest employees. It's even harder to keep them. Take time to praise and cherish your most valuable resources."

M.G.L.J.

STAFFING

Good, dependable employees are crucial for business success. Hence, careful attention needs to be placed on acquiring appropriate, qualified, and reliable personnel. Policies must be developed for every aspect of your business, and personnel is no exception. You can determine your policies once you are in tune with your personality, your likes and dislikes, the objective and nature of your business, and situations that might arise. You also need to consider the different matters which might arise affecting employees and how you wish to handle them. Such policies are considered in the scope of the personnel function, which is wide and varied. It encompasses planning, selection and assignment of employees, performance appraisal, training, development, wage and salary administration, employee benefits, employee services, employee relations, communications, work environment concerns, union relations, reports and record keeping, and equal employment/affirmative action.

When examining specific employee needs, you must determine what jobs are really necessary to accomplish your objectives and then look at the specifics of the job to determine what type of qualifications a person should have for that position. After determining your specific personnel needs, there are different sources from which you can obtain employees, such as the state employment service, private personnel agencies, newspaper ads, and local schools and colleges. Touching base with organizations, associations and people in the community, as well as displaying a sign in your window, are all additional sources from which to obtain employees.

After deciding on the source or sources from which to obtain applicants, some form of screening process needs to be used so that the most appropriate person, based on the needs and desires of the firm, can be selected. It is necessary to develop a good application form in order to obtain all desired information, but make sure that questions are worded clearly and are in accordance with legal constraints (see next page for sample). References from applicants should also be requested. Applicants should, of course, be interviewed to find out as much as possible about the individual. The interview should involve asking specific, well thought-out questions, the answers to which should give enough information about the interviewee to make the decision to hire or not to hire him or her. All applicants being considered for the job should be thoroughly evaluated in terms of the job interview and references before making the hiring decision. Remember, hiring the wrong employee can be very costly and even disastrous, so take time with the hiring process.

APPLICATION FOR EMPLOYMENT

Applicant's Name (Last)	First	Middle Initial	Social Security Number - -
Mailing Address (Number)	Street		Work Telephone Number ( )
City e-mail	State	Zip Code	Home Telephone Number ( )

EDUCATION

Name of School	Location of School	Degree or Course of Study	Date Completed

Please indicate any special abilities, skills, training or relevant certifications that you feel particularly qualify you for the position.

EMPLOYMENT HISTORY – Begin with your most recent job. List each job separately.

Job Title	Dates Worked From ____ To ____	Pay $ ____ Per ____

Name of Employer | *Name of Supervisor*

Address:
City   State   Zip Code

Telephone Number (   )   Reason for Leaving:

Duties Performed:

Job Title	Dates Worked From ____ To ____	Pay $ ____ Per ____

Name of Employer | *Name of Supervisor*

Address:
City   State   Zip Code

Telephone Number (   )   Reason for Leaving:

Duties Performed:

Job Title	Dates Worked From ____ To ____	Pay $ ____ Per ____

Name of Employer | *Name of Supervisor*

Address:
City   State   Zip Code

Telephone Number (   )   Reason for Leaving:

Duties Performed:

May we contact the employers previously listed? ____ If not, indicate which ones you do not wish us to contact.

PERSONAL REFERENCES: List the names of three references that we may contact.

1) Name	Telephone # ( )	Relationship (Teacher etc.)
Address: City	State	Zip Code
2) Name	Telephone # ( )	Relationship (Teacher etc.)
Address: City	State	Zip Code
3) Name	Telephone # ( )	Relationship (Teacher etc.)
Address: City	State	Zip Code

Training

The training aspect of personnel is an area often neglected in terms of importance. The success of a business rests heavily on having qualified, well-trained employees. The nature of training can take a variety of formats, such as on-the-job training, apprenticeships, internships, outside training, vestibule training, classroom training, and a myriad of combinations. Some outside training programs which may be of interest to the entrepreneur include the following:

- Manpower Development Training Act of 1962: Provides federal assistance in training unemployed and underemployed workers. The government reimburses you for part of the wages and training.

- Economic Opportunity Act (Anti-Poverty) of 1964: Firms hire individuals, and the government pays the cost of training.

- The JOBS Program (Job Opportunities in the Business Sector): You submit a proposal for contracts to provide on-the-job training for the disadvantaged employed, and you are paid additional costs incurred because of limited qualifications of those hired and trained.

Considerations in Setting Pay

Employers must address the issue of the level of compensation for their employees.

Factors generally considered are:

- Effort and time required for the job
- The entrepreneur's ability to pay

164

- Cost of living

- Government regulation

- Labor union considerations

- Supply and demand for workers, education level of employees, and industry and area rates

- Incentive plans

- Bonuses based on profit

- Pension plans

Employee Relations

The following guidelines can be used in handling employee grievances effectively:

1. Assure employees that complaining will not prejudice their relationship with their immediate superior.

2. Provide a clear way of presenting grievances.

3. Minimize red tape and time in processing grievances.

4. Provide a way for employees who cannot express themselves easily to present grievances.

All employees should receive a handbook containing major company policies and employee concern areas. A sample table of contents of a typical employee handbook appears on the next page.

EMPLOYEE HANDBOOK

A potential investor, as well as the originator of a business venture, will need to know the key personnel who will be carrying out the objectives of the business. It is necessary for the entrepreneur to pull together a dynamic management and work team who possess the appropriate and necessary skills and knowledge to make the business a success. A good business plan encompasses the resumes of all of the key individuals in charge of operating the business. On the following page you will find a suggested format for including information about all key personnel. Make sure that you capitalize on all skills, experience, and training that directly and indirectly relate to the nature of the proposed venture. Make sure that you have aligned yourself with the right combination of key persons. At this time, you may want to go back to Chapter I and reassess your skills, abilities, and personal characteristics. Make sure that you have personnel who can compensate for your weak areas and strengthen your stronger areas.

Address   Phone, Fax, E-mail

Name

Experience

(List your current or most recent job first; positions held and name of companies; work experience and knowledge in the field of the proposed venture)

Education

(Begin with highest level attained, including schools and year graduated or year training was completed; major and minor courses of study; significant school activities.) Be certain to highlight training relevant to your proposed venture.

Special Skills and/or Certifications

(List all specialized training, skills, and relevant certifications)

Professional Affiliations

(List all professional organizations in which you hold membership)

Community and Civic Affiliations

(List all community involvement and volunteer service activities)

References

(List at least 3 good references, preferably individuals well known in the industry of your proposed business venture or well known in the community, nationally, or locally.)

ENTREPRENEURS

1. What key managerial skills and expertise does the proposed venture need to succeed?

2. Indicate the crucial specialists necessary to consult for success (attorneys, marketing people, accountants).

3. Indicate the primary individuals involved in your firm, including co-founders and their principal skills. Include your own skills and experience with this type of business.

4. List the type of personnel needed for the operation of your business. Include an employee handbook in this section, along with responsibilities of all personnel. (See example of Table of Contents.) All firms, regardless of size, should prepare an employee handbook which summarizes employee-concern areas and policies and serves as an easy reference for the employee as well as the employer.

"When we are foolish, we want to conquer the world.

When we are wise, we want to conquer ourselves."

M.G.L.J.

CHAPTER IX

Organizing Your Business

Details, Details, Details.

"Pay attention to the details even though it may seem that

you are spending too much time on them.

Excellence is in the details."

M.G.L.J.

ORGANIZING YOUR BUSINESS

Regardless of the size of your business venture, there is a need for some systematic way of doing things or some form of organization. A good way of approaching organizational structure is to consider all the activities necessary to accomplish the objectives of the firm. Categorize or put these activities into feasible groupings, and establish appropriate authority for each grouping. The entrepreneur must thoroughly define the personnel required for the accomplishment of the activities of each grouping, prepare an organizational chart, and then thoroughly re-examine all activities and groupings for efficiency and effectiveness.

Such a procedure involves delegation of authority and responsibility. Delegation itself is often difficult for the entrepreneur because it involves letting loose of some of the decision making and control. Nevertheless, proper delegation of authority is necessary for success. One of the main keys to effective delegation is knowing what to delegate and having competent and reliable employees to whom to delegate. With the delegation of authority goes the assignment of responsibility for the completion of the delegated tasks. However, accountability cannot be delegated. The entrepreneur is responsible for the successful operation of the firm, and how successfully the delegated tasks are accomplished will still fall back on the business owner's shoulders. So the importance of competent employees is evident, along with the necessity for a formalized system of control.

Basic Organizing Principles

Two basic organizing principles that will help the entrepreneur to plan the successful operation of the enterprise are:

1. Unity of Command

Employees should have only one superior to whom they are directly responsible.

2. Parity of Authority

Authority should be equal with responsibility. When delegating responsibility, measures must be taken to make sure employees have enough authority to carry out their duties and responsibilities, but not more authority than necessary. Be sure employees have a written statement of their duties, authority, responsibilities, and relationships.

Ways of Organizing Your Business

Seven common ways of structuring a business include organizing by the following:

1. **Function** - similar skills are grouped to form a functional unit

2. **Product** - the business is structured according to the individual services offered to the public.

3. **Process** - similar processes, such as customer service or order processing, are the basis for organizing the firm.

4. **Geographic area** - some firms have locations in different geographical areas and are organized primarily on the basis of territorial concerns.

5. **Type of customers serviced** - some firms service different types of customers, such as wedding consultants and corporate event coordinators, and are structured accordingly.

6. **Project** - some firms, such as consulting businesses, are organized internally based on projects being researched or worked on.

7. **Individual talents of subordinates** - some organizations are structured based on the particular areas of expertise of employees.

Following, you will find a simple organizational chart for a small floral business. This organizational structure shows an obvious, direct relationship between the owner and the customer served. With growth comes the need for a slightly more complex structure and the delegation of duties. The second chart illustrates growth in this firm. As the firm continues to grow, it will become necessary to employ more personnel and distribute more of the duties and responsibilities by creating new positions and/or departments.

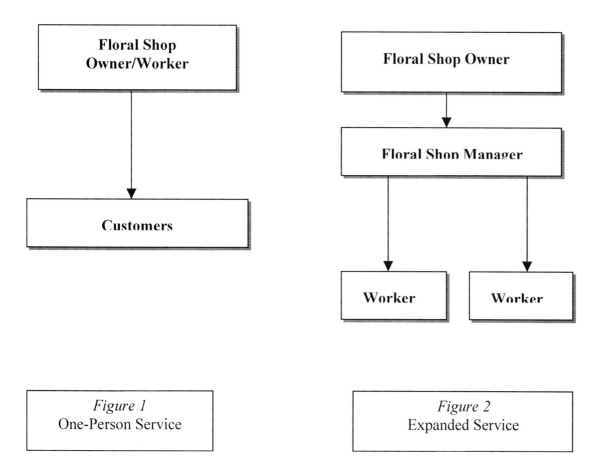

Figure 1
One-Person Service

Figure 2
Expanded Service

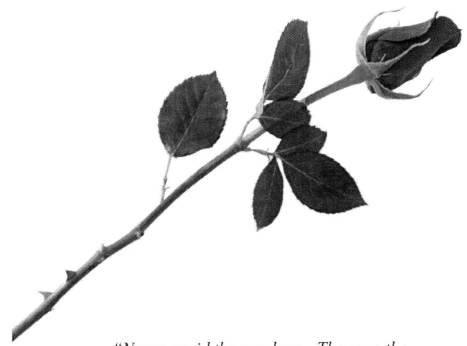

"Never avoid the numbers. They are the

thermometer indicating the health and wealth of your

business."

M.G.L.J.

CHAPTER X

Financing Your Business

"Honesty pays! Get on right and stay on right even when it seems that the smooth, shrewd, fast- talking, and manipulative entrepreneurs are passing you by on the ladder to success. Don't worry; they always eventually miss a step and fall quickly."

M.G.L.J.

FINANCING YOUR BUSINESS

If you are on a limited budget, a good initial strategy is to minimize your outlay on physical items and spend more on equipment, advertising, and your services. All businesses, regardless of the type, will need money to get started and to operate.

After you determine the size of your initial operations, you will have to follow an estimating process of the costs of the essential items and any others appropriate for your establishment. You will need to have enough cash to take care of your operational expenses for several months. Your capital, in essence, should provide enough to keep you going until you can start turning a profit.

The capital you need to be acquiring is often grouped into several categories:

1. Fixed capital: money for the building, equipment, fixtures, and vehicles.

2. Working capital: money for running the business on a day-to-day basis. This covers items such as utilities, money for buying inventory, insurance, advertising, salaries, rent, savings, cash, accounts receivable, etc.

3. Funds for personal living costs: capital to provide for you and your family until the business brings a profit.

4. Money cushion: extra money for unforeseen and unexpected costs.

It is crucial to have sufficient capital. The drawbacks of not having enough capital include:

- business failure

- inability to afford good employees

- investment in sub-standard or inadequate equipment

- inadequate inventory

- inability to obtain a good credit rating

- inability to obtain quantity discounts and other cost advantages

After thoroughly assessing your monetary requirements for starting and operating your venture, you will need to identify sources from which monies can be obtained for starting and operating your enterprise. There are many ways to obtain money to start and operate your business. Business financing is categorized as either **equity** or **debt financing**.

Equity financing represents money which the owner and/or others put into the business. All parties are at risk and at the same time stand to reap rewards. Equity financing is used for starting a business, expanding a business, and financing acquisitions. Equity financing includes personal savings and assets, money from family and friends, investments by key employees, and funds from venture capitalists.

Debt financing, on the other hand, is money loaned to businesses for a fee or interest. The funds borrowed, therefore, must be repaid. Debt financing is also used for business start up, operating funds, and expansion funds. Debt financing includes funds from commercial banks, savings and loans, savings bonds, commercial finance companies, small business investment corporations, federal programs, franchisers, or project organizers.

There are many sources from which funds may be borrowed. They include the following:

Private Investors. Members of the family, friends, business associates, equipment dealers (if the equipment is bought on an installment basis or leased), and wholesalers of products (when they offer 30 to 90 days of credit before demanding payment).

Business Firms. Various business sources, such as:

- Banks

- Savings and loan companies which refinance home mortgages and make property-improvement loans

- Personal finance companies

- Finance companies which provide commercial credit (listed in the yellow pages and advertised in classified and financial sections of newspapers)

- Life insurance companies (some make loans to policy holders)

- Small business investment companies (these companies are licensed by the Small Business Administration to make long-term loans and guarantee bank loans, and they will provide equity financing by actually buying a share of the business)

- Development corporations which are formed by private citizens or businesses to promote the economy in their area

- Venture capital associations or groups of investors looking for businesses with promising futures (they usually provide equity financing, and they often advertise in the classified section of the newspaper want ads and via various Web site listings)

Federal Government. Some of the federal funding sources available are:

- Small Business Administration (SBA)

- Veterans Administration (VA)

Commercial Banks. One of the major sources of borrowing capital is a local commercial bank. It is crucial to have good rapport with your banker. Loans are generally either short-term or long-term in nature. Short-term generally represents money extended for a year or less, and long-term represents money extended for a period over a year. Loans are categorized as secured/collateral loans or unsecured. In the first type, the borrower is asked to pledge something such as life insurance, securities, equipment, real estate, or some other asset belonging to the loan seeker or the business. In the second instance, no security is required; and the loan is made based more on one's financial reputation, managerial ability, bank's evaluation of the business's soundness, etc. Your personal character, business reputation, adequate records, ability to repay the loan, and suitable collateral are all important necessities in obtaining a loan.

Personal Savings, Family and Friends. Your personal savings should be used as a last resort. If you obtain a loan from a bank, always spend the bank's money first.

Friends and family will frequently be receptive to lending you money, particularly if your business plan reflects significant research, and you can convince them that you can give them a greater return on their money than they would be able to obtain from a bank. Be sure when using this form of financing that you protect yourself with a buy-back contract or promissory note at the beginning of the financial relationship. The contract should make it worthwhile for your friends and family to invest in your business. At the same time, it should protect your ownership in the company when you become highly successful. Be cautious with family and friends' financial assistance. Personal relationships can become extremely strained when money is involved.

Life Insurance Policies. Individuals can borrow a major percentage of the cash value of their life insurance policies that have "paid-in" equity. These loan rates are generally much lower than bank loan rates. This form of financing should be investigated if you have such policies, but make sure you know any and all ramifications of borrowing on the equity.

Credit Cards. Credit cards are the most expensive way to finance your business due to the comparatively high interest rates. Try to avoid this form of financing.

Suppliers. Be familiar with all trade credit options. Creative terms with vendors can significantly affect your cash flow so that you have more money available when it is needed. Also, many suppliers, just for the asking, will pay you money if you are using their products. For example, a wholesaler or distributor of imported orchids may compensate you if you advertise that you are the only enterprise offering their exotic florals.

Mortgaging Real Estate. Mortgages on residential property may sometimes be used to finance a business. You should contact your mortgage company for specific information about this form of financing. Be sure to assess the ramifications of using this form of financing, including the fact that you may lose your property if the loan is not repaid in a timely manner.

Savings and Loan Associations. Savings and loan associations historically have specialized in real estate financing, making loans on commercial, industrial, and residential properties. Savings and loan associations are now also beginning to offer the usual type of business loans available through commercial banks.

Venture Capitalists. Venture capitalists are affluent investors who need tax write-offs. They will invest money in your firm in return for your making them limited partners in your business. The majority of all new businesses have losses at first, and some wealthy investors are looking for losses to get tax breaks. You should obtain the assistance of an accountant and attorney before getting involved with venture capitalists.

Small Business Administration. The SBA defines a small business as one that is independently owned and operated and not dominant in its field. They have the specific objective of promoting the small business contribution to the nation's economic growth. By law, they are not allowed to make a loan if the funds can be obtained from a bank or other private source. Therefore, the first step is to try to obtain financing through regular channels. If the loan is turned down, then ask the bank to make the loan under SBA's Loan Guaranty Plan or participate with SBA in a loan. If the banker is interested, ask her or him to contact the SBA to discuss your application. Usually the SBA will deal directly with the banker. The Small Business Administration will consider making a direct loan when these other forms of financing are not obtainable.

Summary of types of loans available from SBA:

1. Guarantee Loan: The SBA will guarantee up to a certain amount of money loaned to a small businessperson.

2. Participation Loan: SBA and the lending institution each put up part of the funds for the loan.

3. Economic Opportunity Loan: The SBA will lend money to any resident of the United States, Puerto Rico, or Guam if:

   a. Total family income from all sources (excluding welfare) is not sufficient for the basic needs of the family, and

   b. Due to social or economic disadvantages, the person has been denied the opportunity to acquire adequate financing through normal channels with reasonable terms. This includes honorably discharged Vietnam-era veterans.

4. Lease Guarantee Program: This is the issuance of an insurance policy or the reinsuring of a policy issued by a private insurance company which guarantees the rent for a small businessperson. A small business is often unable to lease a strategic location because it does not have a prime credit rating as required by some property owners. A guarantee that the rent will not be defaulted on is a valuable negotiating tool in locating a site.

5. Minority Loans: Loans are processed under somewhat relaxed criteria to encourage minority individuals to pursue business ownership.

The SBA also furnishes individual assistance to small businesspersons in the form of counseling, advice, and specific information of various types of business enterprises. The SBA requires all information and an assortment of papers that any other lender would. They will ask the same questions. They require collateral or some other guarantee of repayment, though good character and business ability may weigh more heavily with them than with a bank. However, they do state that the borrower should be able to provide sufficient funds from his or her own resources to have a reasonable amount at stake in the early stages of a new business. Certain SBA loan programs are phased in and others eliminated periodically, so check with your local SBA office for additional information.

Veterans Administration. The purpose of the VA program is to enable the veteran to obtain home, farm or business real estate, supplies and equipment, and working capital. The VA guarantees or insures various types of loans made by private lenders. If you qualify, then the various lenders (banks, savings and loans, etc.) would have to be contacted to determine if they make VA business loans and to set up an appointment. If a loan is not available in this way, the VA can make a direct loan in some cases.

Additional Ways of Obtaining Financing. Various other types of financing are as follows:

1. Financing by selling ownership of the business: Partnership arrangements, corporate arrangements, and public venture capitalists, or small business investment companies

(SBIC's) which are privately owned venture capital firms eligible for federal loans to invest in or lend to businesses.

2. Commercial Finance Companies: Firms which specialize in higher risk loans and generally charge higher interest rates than commercial banks.

3. Consumer Finance Companies: Financing arranged as a personal loan to one or several of the people in the business.

4. Trade Credit: Obtaining credit and financing from suppliers by their extension of terms of payment.

5. Factoring: This form of financing involves the outright sale of a business' accounts receivables to another firm, called a factor. The factor then pays cash to the business for its accounts receivables at a charge for each invoice plus interest on its advance.

Pointers for Successful Debt Financing

- If you are presently working, try to borrow funds while still employed. Studies show that banks are less likely to give you a loan when you do not have a "steady job."

- Make sure that you have devoted great attention to your marketing plan. Bankers want to know that there is actually a substantial market for your business and that you know how to capture the market successfully.

- Be able to sell yourself to the banker, and this includes looking like a businessperson.

- Try to search out a banker who is familiar with your industry.

- Fill out loan documents and applications neatly and accurately.

- Keep trade secrets to yourself. Do not share the details of your unique features unnecessarily. Share enough to establish the fact that you can obtain the competitive edge in the market, but the banker does not need to know everything.

- Under capitalization is a major cause of business failure. Make sure you have accurately assessed your start-up and working capital requirements for at least one year before you initiate your venture. Examine all of the financing sources mentioned in this chapter and determine what is right for you. A sample personal financial statement is included in the appendix to help you determine your personal net worth and assess what collateral you may have to help you find funding for your venture.

CHAPTER XI

Business Records

"Tough times don't last, but tough women do."

M.G.L.J.

BUSINESS RECORDS

The novice entrepreneur probably would want to use the services of an accountant to set up the appropriate business accounting records. The following information is designed to provide you with some insight as to the types of records your accountant should establish, the purpose of each of these records, and the information they should provide you.

Before obtaining funds from whichever source is feasible, it is necessary to have accurate financial records and statements to present to your potential funder. These records are also necessary for successful business operations. Keeping accurate, concise, and appropriate business records is necessary for business success. A great majority of businesses that have failed did not keep accurate records. Good records show whether a business is making a profit, how much profit, and whether the business is efficient and growing. Good records also help you to identify specific problem areas.

For the purpose of efficient business operations as well as funding attainment, all businesses need the following basic financial records:

- **A Record of Cash and Record of Sales Receipts**

- **The Balance Sheet** lists the firm's assets and liabilities. It shows what the business is worth, what the owner owes, and what its obligations are. To be accurate, total assets must equal total liabilities plus owner's equity.

- **The Profit/Loss Statement**, which is often called the **Income Statement,** lists the total sales, cost of goods sold or services rendered, operating expenses, and taxes required in order to obtain a profit, usually for a period of a month. It may take different forms, but is generally a statement of the total amount of goods or services sold less all expenses and costs levied against sales to determine profit or loss from one's operations. Again, this is another statement which helps the entrepreneur determine the efficiency of the business operations and locate problem areas; and it addresses the question of whether or not a profit was made. The most common method of measuring profit is to find out what net profit is, and this is usually calculated on a monthly basis. Net profit is found by taking the total sales for the month and subtracting the cost of sales, which is the total of all expenditures that went directly into whatever was sold.

- **Accounts Payable Record** represents a list of one's suppliers and the amount owed to each.

- **Accounts Receivable Record** shows a list of what each credit customer owes you. It should also show what and when each customer purchases, and is a record of all payments received.

- **Cash Payments Journal** shows all expenditures, including date, expense identity, and reason,

- **Payroll Record** shows gross and net amounts of salaries paid, date of transactions, amount of taxes withheld, and holdings.

- **Schedule of Depreciation** calculates the decrease in value of equipment and furnishings so as to determine net worth. Depreciation schedules are basically lists of the major equipment and furnishings a company owns.

- **Withdrawal and Capital Record** shows what the owner puts in or takes out of the business and serves as a record of transactions which affect ownership.

Good records should show the financial status of the business, trends in the business, and provide important information about your business as well as point to problem areas. The following sample statements, presented in simplistic form, illustrate the usage of several basic records. The actual records and statements for an operating business, of course, will involve more detailed work than these three (3) statements; and again, it is recommended that the services of an experienced accountant be employed.

Elegant Flowers and Gifts
Income Statement
For Month Ended July 31, 20__

Sales		$ 30,000.00
Operating Expenses		
Salaries Expenses	$ 2,000.00	
Rent Expense	700.00	
Automobile Expense	400.00	
Supplies	100.00	
Miscellaneous Expenses	200.00	
Total Operating Expenses		3,400.00
Net Income		$26,600.00

This Income Statement shows the total sales for the month of July, which were $30,000, from which was subtracted the total expenses for that same period, $3,400, thereby providing the total net income for the month of July of $26,600.

Elegant Flowers and Gifts
Capital Statement
For Month Ended July 31, 20__

Capital, July 1, 20___		$10,000.00
Net Income for July	$26,600.00	
Less Withdrawals	2,000.00	
Increase in Capital		24,600.00
Capital, July 31, 20___		34,600.00

The Capital Statement shows the amount of capital the owner had in the business at the beginning of the time period, which was $10,000 on July 1. To this amount is added the net income for the month of July of $26,600 which can be determined by looking at your income statement, less withdrawals of $2,000.00 yielding an increase in capital of $24,600. The increase in capital for the month of July added to the beginning capital gives the total capital position at the end of the month of $34,600.

Elegant Flowers and Gifts
Balance Sheet
July 31, 20__

Assets

Cash	$18,600.00
Accounts Receivable	15,000.00
Supplies	3,000.00
Total Assets	36,600.00

Liabilities

Accounts Payable	$ 2,000.00

Capital

Elegant Expressions,Captital	$34,600.00
Total Liabilities & Capital	$36,600.00

The Balance Sheet visually depicts the accounting equation: **Assets = Liabilities + Owner's Equity**. This statement lists the firm's total assets as of July 31, which were $36,600, along with the total liabilities or total debt of the firm of $2,000, and the owner's capital of $34,600.

$$A = L + OE$$
Assets = Liabilities + Capital or Owner's Equity

$$\$36,600 = \$2,000.00 + \$34,600$$

A potential financier for a new business will be particularly interested in the following information and statements:

1. Start-Up Costs (Estimated)

2. Owner's Living Expenses (Estimated)

3. Operating Costs (Projected)

4. Balance Sheet (Projected)

5. Profit/Loss (Income) Statement (Projected)

6. Cash Flow Statement (Projected)

7. Break-Even Analysis

The small business owner on a daily basis should:

1. Check cash on hand.

2. Check the bank balance.

3. Check the daily summary of sales and cash receipts.

4. Make sure that all errors in recording collections on accounts are corrected.

5. Make sure that a record of all monies paid out, by cash or check, is maintained.

The small business owner on a weekly basis should:

1. Check accounts receivable, and take action on delinquent accounts.

2. Check accounts payable, and take advantage of discounts for early payment.

3. Make sure payroll records are in order.

4. Make sure taxes and reports to State and Federal Government are prepared and sent.

The small business owner on a monthly basis should:

1. Make sure that all Journal entries are posted to the General Ledger.

2. Assess the Profit/Loss Statement.

3. Assess the Balance Sheet.

4. Make sure the Bank Statement is reconciled.

5. Make sure the Petty Cash Account is in balance.

6. Make sure that all Federal Tax Deposits, Withheld Income and FICA Taxes (Form 501) and State Taxes are made.

7. Make sure that Accounts Receivable are aged, i.e., 30, 60, 90 days, etc., and collect past dues.

8. Check inventory.

"It's not the one who falls that fails, but the one who falls,

gives up, and never gets up."

M.G.L.J.

CHAPTER XII

Sales Forecasting

"Trying times are times for trying new ideas."

M.G.L.J.

SALES FORECASTING

Once the decision has been made to go into business and the type of business has been selected, the next step is to forecast sales of goods or services for at least the first year. This is not an easy task, as you are dealing with many unknown factors; nevertheless, it is necessary to attempt to make an intelligent forecast using sound rationale. Sales forecasting requires you to predict the future as accurately as possible with justification for the forecasted figures. A forecast can be based on your personal judgment, interviews with people operating similar businesses, various types of published data, information from experts, as well as market calculations. Factors to take into consideration when forecasting sales include industry trends for your area; forecasts for retail floral businesses in your state, city, and area; and an assessment of your competition.

One approach to developing a sales forecast begins by estimating the total number of persons in the selected target market. This estimate comes from an analysis of your market via a survey and also from secondary sources such as **Statistical Abstracts of the U. S.**, marketing and demographic informational sources, and industry publications.

The following four equations will allow you to forecast sales:

(1) T x A = TPM

(2) TPM x P = TAM

(3) TAM x EMS = Sales in Units

(4) Sales in Units x PR = Sales in Dollars

Explanation:

(1) T x A = TPM

Total number of people in the target market multiplied by the annual number of purchases per person = total potential market.

(2) TPM x P = TAM

Total potential market multiplied by the percent of the total market coverage you think you might be able to obtain = total available market.

(3) TAM x EMS = Sales in Units

Total available market multiplied by the expected market share you expect to obtain = sales forecast in units.

(4) Sales in Units x PR = Sales in Dollars

Sales forecast in units multiplied by the price per unit = sales forecast in dollars.

When determining your expected market share, be sure to take into consideration the present market share of your competitors, the amount of promotion you will be using compared to your competition, the sales trends of similar services, and what the present competition may do to improve their present service when you enter the market.

CHAPTER XIII

The Investment Prospectus

"There is no escalator to success. You have to walk the stairs."

M.G.L.J.

THE INVESTMENT PROSPECTUS

All important information about your business can strategically and, for impact purposes, be summarized in an investment prospectus. Someone considering investing in your business or lending you money wants to know exactly and quickly how much money you need and why they should lend it to you. (How profitable is it going to be?) Profit is important to an investor; however, many individuals considering venture initiation get entwined in the development of their idea into a business and fail to look at how profitable it stands to be. An outline of an investment prospectus follows.

Investment Prospectus Outline

Cover letter describing:
    Nature of business
    Amount of financing needed
    Terms of loan

Business description:
    Name and location
    Nature of business
    Organizational structure
    Product or service description
    Business goals
    Summary of financial needs and proposed use of funds

Market strategy:
    Market analysis
    Target market
    Competition
    Marketing objectives
    Price policies
    Distribution system
    Promotion

Production:
    Suppliers
    Production methods

Product services
Patents, legal, and technical information

Management:
    Management/ownership structure
    Education and work experience of board of directors and key personnel
    Personnel plan
    Compensation policy

Financial data:
    Financial statements
    Profit and loss statements (monthly for one year with explanation of projections)
    Balance sheets (projected one year after loan or investment with explanation of projections)
    Cash flow projection (monthly for one year with explanation of projections)
    Specific uses of investment funds
    Credit references

CHAPTER XIV

Is It Feasible?

"If the word QUIT is part of your vocabulary, then the

word FINISH is likely not."

Anonymous

IS IT FEASIBLE?

Your final considerations should address whether or not your proposed venture is feasible. Be sure you reiterate all significant justifications in this section.

The SBA provides a convenient checklist for those going into business. The following checklist affords a good opportunity to go back and make sure you have considered all necessary factors. Answer each question with a yes/no response. Then go back and evaluate your responses throughout the entire publication and determine if your considered business venture is feasible and has a significant chance for success.

YOU

Are you the kind of person who can get a business started and make it go?

_____ Think about why you want to own your own business. Do you want a business badly enough to work long hours without knowing how much money you will end up with?

_____ Have you worked in a business like the one you want to start?

_____ Have you worked for someone else as a supervisor or manager?

_____ Have you had any business training in school?

_____ Have you saved any money?

MONEY

_____ Do you know how much money you will need to get your business started?

_____ Have you counted how much of your own money you can put into the business?

_____ Do you know how much credit you can get from your suppliers?

_____ Do you know where you can borrow the rest of the money you need to start your business?

_____ Have you figured out what net income per year you can expect to get from the business? Count your salary and your profit on the money you put into the business.

_____ Can you live on less than that amount so that you can use some of it to help your business grow?

_____ Have you talked to a banker about your plans?

FORM OF BUSINESS

_____ If you need a partner with money or know-how that you do not have, do you know someone appropriate who is someone you can get along with?

_____ Do you know the good and bad points about going into business alone, having a partner and incorporating your business?

_____ Have you talked with a lawyer about the appropriate form of ownership?

CUSTOMERS OR CLIENTS

_____ Do most businesses in your community seem to be doing well?

_____ Have you tried to find out whether enterprises like the one you want to open are doing well in your community and in the rest of the country?

_____ Do you know what kind of people will want to buy what you plan to sell?

_____ Do people who would want your product live in the area where you want to open your business?

_____ Do they need a business like yours?

_____ If not, have you thought about opening a different kind of enterprise or going to another neighborhood?

YOUR BUILDING

_____ Have you found a good building for your business?

_____ Will you have enough room when your business gets bigger?

_____ Can you fix the building the way you want it without spending too much money?

_____ Can people get to it easily from parking spaces, bus stops, or their homes?

_____ Have you had a lawyer check the lease and zoning restrictions?

EQUIPMENT AND SUPPLIES

_____ Do you know just what equipment and supplies you need and how much they will cost?

YOUR SERVICE

_____ Have you decided what services you will sell?

_____ Have you found suppliers who will sell you what you need at a good price?

_____ Have you compared the prices and credit terms of different suppliers?

YOUR RECORDS

_____ Have you planned a system of records that will keep track of your income and expenses, what you owe other people, and what other people owe you?

_____ Have you worked out a way to keep track of your supply inventory so that you will always have enough on hand?

_____ Have you figured out how to keep your payroll records and handle tax reports and payments?

_____ Do you know what financial statements you should prepare?

_____ Do you know how to use these financial statements?

_____ Do you know an accountant to help you with your records and financial statements?

YOUR BUSINESS AND THE LAW

_____ Do you know what licenses and permits you need?

_____ Do you know what business laws you have to obey?

_____Do you know a lawyer you can go to for advice and for help with legal papers?

PROTECTING YOUR BUSINESS

_____Have you made plans for protecting your business against thefts of all kinds--
shoplifting, robbery, burglary, employee stealing?

_____Have you talked with an insurance agent about what kinds of insurance you need?

BUYING A BUSINESS SOMEONE ELSE HAS STARTED

_____ Have you made a list of what you like and do not like about buying a business someone
else has started?

_____ Are you sure you know the real reason why the owner wants to sell the business?

_____ Have you compared the cost of buying the business with the cost of starting a new firm?

_____ Are the supplies and inventory in good condition?

_____ Is the building in good condition?

_____ Will the owner of the building transfer the lease to you?

_____ Have you talked with other businesspersons in the area to see what they think of the
business?

_____ Have you talked with the company's suppliers?

_____ Have you talked with a lawyer about it?

CHAPTER XV
Conclusion

"Never give up on your dream just because it's taking too long for it

to become a reality. The time will pass anyway, so you might as well

be working on realizing your dream."

M.G.L.J.

MAKING IT GO

The following considerations are presented to assist you in making a more thorough assessment of the feasibility of your business concept.

ADVERTISING

- ❑ Have you decided how you will advertise? (Newspapers, Web site, posters, handbills, radio, direct mail, etc.)

- ❑ Do you know where to get help with your ads?

- ❑ Have you watched what other businesses similar to yours do to get people to buy?

THE PRICES YOU CHARGE

- ❑ Do you know how to figure what you should charge for each service you sell?

- ❑ Do you know what other enterprises like yours charge?

BUYING

- ❑ Do you have a plan for finding out what your customers want?

- ❑ Will your plan for keeping track of your inventory tell you when it is time to order more and how much to order?

- ❑ Do you plan to fill most of your needs from a few suppliers rather than a little from many, so that those you buy from will want to help you succeed?

SELLING

- ❑ Do you know how to get customers to buy?

- ❑ Have you thought about why you like to buy from some sales representatives while others turn you off?

YOUR EMPLOYEES

❑ If you need to hire someone to help you, do you know where to look?

❑ Do you know what kind of person you need?

❑ Do you know how much to pay?

❑ Do you have a plan for training your employees?

CREDIT FOR YOUR CUSTOMERS OR CLIENTS

❑ Have you decided whether to let your customers buy on credit?

❑ Do you know the advantages and disadvantages of joining a credit card plan?

❑ Can you tell a deadbeat from a good credit customer?

A FEW EXTRA QUESTIONS

❑ Have you figured out whether you could make more money working for someone else?

❑ Does your family support your plan to start a business of your own?

❑ Do you know where to find out about new ideas and new services?

❑ Do you have a work plan for yourself and your employees?[19]

❑ Have you considered business regulations and insurance? Please reflect on the following.

REGULATIONS

Every potential business owner must become familiar with the different business regulations and laws affecting her or his type of business and, specifically, her or his area as they vary from locality to locality. These laws change from time to time so it is necessary to obtain current information for your locality. The licenses and permits required to start a business vary among cities, counties, and states. The individual considering entrepreneurship should consult local government agencies or the local Chamber of Commerce for this type of information.

INSURANCE

Many businesses fail each year due to natural disasters, fire, damage suits, burglary, death of a partner, vandalism, employee theft, fraud, etc. Different types of insurance exist which can cover all of these different situations to minimize your risk. It is best to contact a reputable insurance company for your particular needs. Five kinds of insurance are essential: fire insurance, liability insurance, automobile insurance, workers' compensation, and crime insurance. Based on your particular business, you may need many additional types of insurance coverage. A good insurance company will be able to advise you as to appropriate coverage. Also, consult a good attorney for advice on the appropriate insurance coverage for your business.

The operation of the proposed venture must be examined to determine if the sale of the product or service at certain cost levels seems feasible. The following concerns should be considered:

1. What are the major difficulties in the sale of the product or delivery of the service being considered?

2. Why do you think you can sell the venture's product or operate your service at competitive cost level?

3. Discuss the layout of your firm in terms of physical facilities.

4. Thoroughly consider and discuss all major risks and problems and address the minimization of the serious risks.

If you decide that your business is feasible, additional steps need to be taken in order to officially begin operations.

You should.....

- Obtain a business license from the city and/or county clerk.

- Obtain an employee federal identification number from the nearest Internal Revenue Service Office.

- Obtain an application for a sales and use tax certificate of registration.

- Comply with appropriate local, state, and federal regulations.

- State laws require employers to cover employees with workers' compensation insurance. Contact the State Department of Labor and obtain the form "First Report of Work Insurance" to determine your state requirements.

- Comply with the requirements of your State Division of Occupational and Health Association even if you employ only one person.

- Determine if certification by an appropriate board is required for your business.

- Contact your State Regulatory Board for necessary details.

- Check into local permits and ordinances.

- Check with your local or state Small Business Office or local Small Business Development Center to make sure you are in compliance with the regulations for your state and local municipality.

POINTERS FOR BUSINESS SUCCESS

This writer would like to close this publication with a few last pointers for small business success.

1. Develop a "total product" desired by the appropriate target market.

2. Please your customers.

    - Learn their likes and dislikes and make them feel that you are interested.

    - Given an extra bit of service, people will tell others.

    - It is the little things that count and that give your clients or customers that "warm and fuzzy" feeling, and keeps them coming back.

    - Tell the truth about your service even if it means losing a sale. Telling the truth will make that "would be" customer feel that you are an honest businessperson, and they will perhaps patronize you later or tell others.

    - Build an image.

    - Use a steady promotion plan and be consistent in everything you do.

3. Encourage teamwork.

    - Make employees feel that they are important to your business.

    - Praise employees in public; correct them in private.

    - Send your staff to workshops and seminars periodically. The knowledge obtained will allow them to benefit your organization more; and at the same time, it will elevate their feeling of worth to you and your organization.

4. Plan ahead.

5. Keep expenses in line and make a profit. Determine your break-even point.

6. Be involved in civic and community affairs. This is free advertising. Do benevolent community deeds which will bring a positive valence to your firm.

7. Keep your firm's name in the public's eye.

    ▪ Always carry your business cards and brochures.

    ▪ Have your business checks imprinted with your logo and a descriptive statement about your business. Checks pass through the hands of many individuals who may be in your target market.

8. Interact and socialize with people who can help you with your business concerns. "It's not what you know; it's who you know." This is an old cliche, but it is quite true in the world of small business. Particularly get to know a banker, lawyer, accountant, marketing/promotion specialist, local politicians, news media representatives, leaders of business, civic, service, political, educational, religious, and professional organizations, and the decision makers of the companies with whom you do business. You may also want to consider joining your local Chamber of Commerce.

9. Establish yourself as an authority in your field or industry. Use your contacts and get on the guest lecture circuit, talk shows, and community programs. You may even want to teach a class in your field as a part of the continuing education program of a local college. You may have to offer your teaching free initially, but the benefits derived will be great.

10. Establish credibility for your business.

11. Provide a good service at an acceptable price and back up your product with guarantees and warranties.

12. Live up to the commitments you make.

13. Surround yourself with people who know more than you do. Hire staff personnel whose areas of expertise will enable you to expand your knowledge as well as expand your business.

14. Establish and maintain good credit.

15. Pay your bills on time. If you can't pay on time, call your creditor and see what other arrangements can be made. (These bills will not disappear, so face up to the problem which is quite common for small businesses.)

16. Take advantage of early payment discounts and quantity discounts whenever possible.

17. Always represent your business in a very professional manner.

   - You are your business, and people will evaluate your business based on you. Your personal appearance is very important at all times, even on Saturday morning in the grocery store.

   - Always wear clothes that are appropriate for your business field and that make you feel that you look good. You feel and act like you look.

   - When greeting people, always use a firm, confident handshake with direct eye contact and a friendly smile.

18. Keeping cash flow concerns in mind, establish a feasible credit policy for customers and clients.

CHAPTER XVI

Business Glossary

"Keep your eye on the prize--your entrepreneurial dream.

There are very few joys as wonderful as the joy of loving what you do

every day and getting paid for it."

M.G.L.J.

BUSINESS GLOSSARY

ANGELS	People who may be willing to supply capital to an entrepreneur with no strings attached. These individuals may include relatives, friends, or a mentor.
ASSET	An item of value owned by a business or individual.
BALANCE SHEET	A financial statement which lists the firm's assets and liabilities. It shows what the business is worth.
BALLOON PAYMENT	A final payment, generally on an installment loan, that is larger than the preceding payment.
BANKRUPT	The state of a person or firm unable to pay creditors and judged legally insolvent.
BOND	A long-term instrument used to finance the capital needs of a business or government unit.
BREAK-EVEN POINT	The volume of sales at which the firm's costs equal its income. Above the break-even point, a firm is making money. Below the break-even point, a firm is losing money.
BROKER	An agent who negotiates contracts of purchase or sale but does not take control of the goods.
BUDGET	An itemized summary of probable expenditures and income for a given period of time with a plan for meeting expenses.
BUSINESS PLAN	Document prepared by the business owners which details specific information about the firm.
BUYER	The person who makes the purchase decisions for a firm.
COLLATERAL	Property, stocks, bonds, savings accounts, life insurance, and current business assets which may be held to insure repayment of a loan.

CAPITAL	Cash or cash equivalents necessary to fund a business entity.
CAPITAL ASSET	An asset with a life of more than one year that is not bought and sold in the ordinary course of business activity.
CAPITAL BUDGETING	The process of planning expenditures on assets whose returns are expected to extend beyond one year.
CAPITAL GAINS (LOSSES)	Profits (or losses) on the sale of capital assets owned for six months or more.
CASH FLOW	A financial projection utilized by business owner(s) to evaluate receipts and disbursements over time. A cash forecast is used to predict high and low points in regard to profitability.
CASH FLOW PROJECTION	Forecast of the cash a business anticipates receiving and distributing during the course of a given span of time.
CASH MANAGEMENT	The practice of using the firm's money to earn money rather than allowing it to remain in accounts which do not pay interest.
COMMERCIAL BANK	An ordinary bank of deposit and discount, with checking accounts, as distinguished from a savings bank.
COMMON STOCK	The ownership element of a corporation represented by shares of stock.
COMPETITIVE EDGE	A particular characteristic (or characteristics) which makes a firm and/or product more attractive to customers than its competitors.
CONSIGNMENT	Goods placed by the supplier in the inventory of the consignee. The consignee pays the supplier only when goods are sold.
CONSUMER GOODS	Goods which are bought by the final user.

CONSUMER PRODUCT SAFETY COMMISSION	A federal commission with responsibility for establishing product safety standards and for taking appropriate steps to reduce unreasonable risks of injury or harm to consumers.
CONTINGENCY FUND	Monies set aside for unexpected expenditures.
CORPORATION	A form of business ownership which is considered a legal entity separate and distinct from the owner.
COST-BENEFIT ANALYSIS	An analytic technique of weighing the costs of a project or investment against the benefits derived from it.
COTTAGE INDUSTRY	Another term for the home-based business industry.
CPA	Certified Public Accountant.
CREDIT POLICIES	The firm's customer-payment policies.
DEBT CAPITAL	Monies loaned to the business owner which are used to increase and enhance the value of the firm. The money plus interest must be repaid over time and represents a debt for the firm.
DEBT FINANCING	Funds borrowed for certain business purposes and which must be repaid by the business to the lender.
DECENTRALIZATION	The degree to which decision making has been delegated downward in the organization.
DISPOSABLE INCOME	Personal income remaining after the deduction of taxes on personal income and other compulsory payments.
DROP SHIPMENT	The delivery of goods directly from a producer or wholesaler to the consumer.
DUN & BRADSTREET	A mercantile agency which offers credit ratings, financial analysis, and other financial services, usually on a contractual basis.
EBIT	Earnings before interest and taxes.

EMPLOYEE TURNOVER	The rate at which employees are hired and terminated, or leave the organization.
ENTREPRENEUR	A person who organizes, manages, and initiates a business venture.
EQUITY	The net worth of a business which consists of capital stocks, capital (or paid-in) surplus, earned surplus (or retained earnings), and, sometimes, certain net worth reserves.
EQUITY CAPITAL	Money obtained by selling a part of the interest in the business.
FRANCHISOR	The owner of the product or service in a franchising relationship.
FRANCHISEE	The affiliated dealer through which a franchisor distributes products or services.
FRANCHISING	A form of licensing by which the owner of a product, service, or process obtains distribution at the retail level through affiliated dealers.
FIXED ASSETS	Assets of a business which are relatively permanent and are necessary for the functioning of the firm. Fixed assets include buildings, furniture, equipment, etc.
FIXED COSTS	Costs which remain constant regardless of changes in output. Fixed costs include interest on long-term loans, rents, salaries, etc.
FOB (FREE ON BOARD)	The point at which the title of goods transfers (free on board) from the producer to the buyer. FOB origin means that the title is transferred upon leaving the loading dock of the producer and that the shipping costs are paid by the buyer.
GENERAL PARTNERSHIP	A partnership arrangement in which each partner is held liable for the acts of other partners.

GOOD FAITH	A sincere belief that the accomplishment intended is not unlawful or harmful to another.
GOODS-IN-PROCESS	Goods in the midst of production or manufacture such that they are neither in a raw material state nor finished.
GOODWILL	Intangible asset based on the good image of a firm and established by the excess of the price paid for the going concern over its book value.
GROSS INCOME	Amount received by the firm before deducting operating expenses.
HOME-BASED BUSINESS	A business primarily operating out of the owner's or owners' home(s).
IMPULSE GOODS	Goods bought by consumers on sight to satisfy a desire that is strongly felt at the moment.
INVENTORY	The total of items of tangible property which a firm uses up or sells during a short time, including goods, material, supplies, and tools.
INVESTMENT PROSPECTUS	A document which highlights the major information regarding a business. This document summarizes information so that potential investors can quickly and easily evaluate a business venture.
INVESTMENT TAX CREDIT	A credit from federal income taxes that is computed as a percentage of the initial cost of certain capital assets.
JOBBER	A wholesaler or distributor.
LIABILITY	A debt or obligation of a business.
LIMITED PARTNER	The liability of the limited partner is limited to the amount he or she contributes to the enterprise owned.

LIMITED PARTNERSHIP	A partnership arrangement which is created by compliance with a state's statutory requirements. It is composed of one or more persons. One partner must be a general partner.
LINE AND STAFF	A descriptive term which defines the structure of an organization. Line refers to jobs or roles which have direct authority and responsibility for output. Staff personnel contribute indirectly or support line personnel.
LINE OF CREDIT	An arrangement whereby a financial institution commits itself to lend to a firm or individual up to a specified maximum amount of funds during a specified period.
LIQUIDATION	The process of terminating a firm's existence by selling its assets and paying its debts.
LIQUIDITY	A firm's cash position and its ability to meet maturing obligations.
LOSS LEADER	A product priced at a loss or no profit for the purpose of attracting patronage to a store.
MBO (MANAGEMENT BY OBJECTIVES)	A management technique of defining attainable goals for subordinates through an agreement of the supervisor and subordinates. It offers continual feedback to subordinates in terms of their contribution to the organization's total performance.
MANUFACTURER'S AGENT	An agent who generally operates on an extended contractual basis, often sells a definite portion of the principal's output within an exclusive territory, handles noncompeting but related lines of goods, and possesses limited authority with regard to prices and terms of sales.
MARKDOWN	A reduction in selling price. (An item priced at $1 would have a 30 percent markdown if it were discounted to a special price of $0.70.)

MARKET SEGMENTATION	A marketing strategy consciously developed to produce a product or service that embodies characteristics preferred by a selected small part of a total market.
MARKET SHARE	The percentage of the total market that the firm can obtain.
MARKETING	Activities concerned with the sale and distribution of a firm's products and/or services according to needs of customers.
MARKETING CHANNEL	The pipeline through which a product flows on its way to the ultimate consumer.
MARKETING CONCEPT	The way in which a firm chooses to give special consideration to the needs, desires and wishes of prospective and present customers.
MARKETING MIX	A blend in the proper proportions of the basic elements of product, price, promotion, and place into an integrated marketing program.
MARKETING PLAN	A plan which details the marketing activity and marketing direction a firm plans to take.
MISSION	The long-term vision of what the firm is trying to become.
NET PROFIT	The amount earned by the firm after paying operating expenses and taxes.
NET WORTH	The difference between assets and liabilities.
OBJECTIVES	Purposes, goals, and desired results for the company and its parts.
ODD PRICING	Setting the price of goods to end in an odd number (such as $9.95).
OPERATING EXPENSES	General expenses incurred by the business to generate sales.

OVERHEAD	All the costs of a business other than direct labor and materials.
OWNER'S EQUITY	The amount of cash or other assets the owner has invested in the business.
PARTNERSHIP	The joining of two or more individuals to form an organization.
PAYBACK PERIOD	The length of time required for the net revenues of an investment to equal the cost of the investment.
POLICIES	Overall guides for action and decision making to provide some consistency in company operations.
PREFERRED STOCK	A type of company financing that has characteristics of both bonds and common stock.
PRICE/ EARNINGS RATIO	The ratio of price per share to earnings per share.
PRIVATE BRAND	A brand sponsored by a merchant (e.g., Kroger) or agent as distinguished from brands sponsored by manufacturers or producers.
PRODUCT LINE	A group of products that are closely related because they satisfy a class of needs, are used together, are sold to the same customer groups, are marketed through the same type of outlet, or fall within a given price range.
PROFIT-LOSS STATEMENT	Also called the Income Statement, this financial statement lists the total sales, cost of goods sold, expenses, and taxes required in order to obtain a profit (usually for a period of a month).
PROMOTION	A blend of the three following sales activities: (l) mass, impersonal selling efforts (advertising), (2) personal sales, and (3) other activities, such as point-of-purchase displays, shows, or exhibits.
PROPRIETORSHIP	An enterprise owned by one individual. The owner and the business are one and the same and cannot be legally distinguished and separated by law.

RETAILER	A merchant or agent whose main business is to buy goods for resale to the ultimate consumer.
SAVINGS AND LOAN BANK	A bank which accepts and pays interest on deposit savings, subject to conditions prescribed by the Federal Home Loan Bank Board.
SBA	Small Business Administration. The SBA is the major governmental agency formulated to assist small businesses.
SBDC	Small Business Development Center. SBDCs are established to provide free management assistance to small business owners.
SERVICE BUSINESS	A firm filling non-product needs of customers. (Examples are banking and repairing firms.)
SILENT PARTNER	An investor who does not have any management responsibilities but provides capital and shares liability for any losses experienced by the entity. (Also known as a sleeping partner.)
SPAN OF CONTROL	The number of subordinates reporting to one supervisor in an organization.
SPECIALTYGOODS	Items which are bought infrequently at particular outlets after a special effort.
STRATEGY	A plan of action to attain specified objectives.
STRATEGIC PLAN	A major, comprehensive, long-term plan providing direction for a firm to accomplish its mission and objectives.
TARGET MARKET	The group of people to whom a firm directs its marketing efforts.
TRADE ASSOCIATION	An organization formed to benefit members of the same trade by informing and supporting its members.

TRADE CREDIT	Inter firm debt arising through credit sales and recorded as an account receivable by the seller and as an account payable by the buyer.
TRADEMARK	A name or logo which is given legal protection because it refers exclusively to a product. It may be used only by the trademark owner.
UNDER- CAPITALIZATION	The lack of funds necessary to optimally start and operate a venture.
UNITY OF COMMAND	The theory that an employee should have only one superior to whom he or she is directly responsible for certain matters.
VENTURE CAPITAL	Cash or cash equivalents supplied by an outside party who specializes in providing working capital for small and/or growing businesses. Venture capitalists require an equity interest in the firm in return for supplying capital assistance.
WHOLESALER	A business unit which buys and resells merchandise to retailers and other merchants and/or to industrial, institutional, and commercial users but which does not sell in significant amounts to ultimate consumers.
WORKING CAPITAL	Current assets less current liabilities.

CHAPTER XVII

Business
Resources

"By perseverance, the tortoise won the race."

M.G.L.J.

FLORAL ASSOCIATIONS

American Institute of Floral Designers	720 Light Street Baltimore, MD 21230 Phone:(410) 752-3318 www.AIFD.org
Extra Touch Florist Association	197 Woodlawn Parkway Suite 104-280 San Marcos, CA 92069 Phone: 1-888-419-1515 (Toll Free) Fax: (323) 657-5379 www.etfassociation.org
FTD, Inc.	3113 Woodcreek Drive Downers Grove, IL 60515 Phone: 1-800-788-9000 www.FTD.com www.FTDI.com
Society of American Florists	1601 Duke Street Alexandria, VA 22314 1-800-336-4743 Phone: (703) 836-8700 www.SAFNOW.org
Teleflora Delivery Service (TDS)	Teleflora P.O. BOX 60910 Los Angeles, CA 90060 - 0910 Phone: 1-800-898-7484 www.teleflora.com
Wholesale Florist & Florist Supplier Association	147 Old Solomons Island Road, Suite 302 Annapolis, MD 21401 Phone: 1-888-289-3372 (Toll Free) Phone: (410) 573-0400 Fax: (410) 573-5001 www.wffsa.org

FLORAL PERIODICALS

FLORAL MANAGEMENT	Floral Management Magazine The Society of American Florists 1601 Duke Street Alexandria, VA 22314 Phone: (703) 836-8700 Fax: (703) 836-8705 www.safnow.org Monthly
FLORISTS' REVIEW	Florists' Review Enterprises, Inc. P.O.B. 4368 Topeka, KS 66604 Phone: 1-800-367-4708 Phone: (785) 266-0888 www.floristsreview.com Monthly
FLOWER NEWS	Central Flower News, Inc. 205 W. Wacker Dr. Suite 1040 Chicago, IL 60006 Phone: 1-800-732-4581 Phone: (312) 739-5000 www.flowernews.com Weekly
TELEFLORA'S SPIRIT	Teleflora P.O. BOX 60910 Los Angeles, CA 90060 - 0910 Phone: 1-800-898-7484 www.teleflora.com Monthly
WF&FSA's Buyer's Guide and Membership Directory	Wholesale Florist & Florist Supplier Association 147 Old Solomons Island Road, Suite 302 Annapolis, MD 21401 Phone: 1-888-289-3372 (Toll Free) Phone: (410) 573-0400 Fax: (410) 573-5001 www.wffsa.org

GIFT ASSOCIATIONS

American Craft Council	72 Spring Street 6th Floor New York, NY 10012-4019 Phone: (212) 274-0630 Fax: (212) 274-0650 www.craftcouncil.org
American Assn. of Exporters and Importers	1200 G Street, NW Suite 800 Washington, DC 20005 Phone: (202) 661-2181 Fax. (202) 661-2185 www.aaei.org/about/contact.html
Art Glass Association	PO Box 2537 Zanesville, OH 43702-2537 Phone:(740) 454-1194 Phone: (866) 301-2421 (Toll Free) Fax: (740) 454-1194 www.artglassassociation.com
Assn. of Bridal Consultants (ABC)	200 Chestnutland Rd. New Milford, CT 06776-2521 Phone: (860) 355-0464 Fax: (860) 354-1404 www.bridalassn.com
The Balloon Council (TBC)	512 11th St. SE Washington, DC 20003 Phone: 1-800-233-8887 www.balloonhq.com/BalloonCouncil/about.html
Color Marketing Group (CMG)	5845 Richmond Hwy., #410 Alexandria, VA 22303, USA Phone: (703) 329-8500 Fax: (703) 329-0155 cmg@colormarketing.org

Direct Marketing Assn. (DMA)	1120 Avenue of the Americas New York, NY 10036-6700 Phone: (212) 768-7277 Fax: (212) 302-7643 www.the-dma.org
The Gift Association of America (GAA)	115 Rolling Hills Road Johnstown, PA 15095-5225 Phone: (814) 288-1460 Fax: (814) 288-1483 www.giftassn.com
Gift for Life	120 Wall Street, 13th Floor New York, NY 10005 Phone: (212) 806-1600 Fax: (212) 806-1601 www.giftforlife.org
Gifts & Decorative Accessories	360 Park Avenue South, New York, NY 10010 Phone: (646) 746-6400 Fax: (646) 746-7431 www.giftsanddec.com
Greeting Card Assn. (GCA)	1030 15th St. NW Suite 870 Washington, DC 20005 Phone: (202) 393-1778 Fax: (202) 393-0336 E-mail: gca@rgminc.com www.greetingcard.org
Hobby Industry Assn.	319 E 54th St. PO Box 348 Elmwood Park, NJ 07307 Phone: (201) 794-1133 Fax: (201) 797-0657 E-mail: hia@ix.netcom.com www.hobby.org

International Licensing Industry Merchandisers' Assn. (LIMA)	350 Fifth Ave., Suite 2309 New York, NY 10118-0110 Phone: (212) 244-1944 Fax: (212) 563-6552 www.licensing.org
National Assn. of Limited Edition Dealers (NALED)	National Headquarters 332 Hurst Mill North Bremen, GA 30110 Phone: 1-800-HI-NALED (1-800-446-2533) Phone: (770) 537-1970 www.naled.com
National Assn. of Wholesaler-Distributors	1725 K St. Washington, DC 20006 Phone: (202) 872-0885 Fax: (202) 785-0586 www.naw.org
National Candle Assn.	1156-15th Street NW, Suite 900 Washington, DC 20005 Phone: (202) 393-2210 Fax: (202) 393-0336 www.candles.org
The National NeedleArts Assn. (TNNA)	PO Box 3388 Zanesville, OH 43702-3388 Phone: 1-800-889-8662 Phone: (740) 455-6773 Fax: (740) 452-2552 www.tnna.org
National Retail Federation	325 7th St NW 1100 Washington DC 20004 Phone: 1-800-NRF-HOW2 Fax: 202-737-2849 www.nrf.com

Society of Glass and Ceramic Decorators (SGCD)	47 N. Fourth Street / PO Box 2489, Zanesville, OH 43702 Phone: (740) 588-9882 Fax: 740-588-0245 www.sgcd.org
United Assn. Manufacturers' Representatives	PO Box 986 Dana Point, CA 92629 Phone: (949) 240-4966 Fax: (949) 240-7001 E-mail: uamr@pacbell.net www.uamr.com

GIFT PERIODICALS

Balloons & Parties

PartiLife Publications, L.L.C.
65 Sussex Street
Hackensack, NJ 07601
Phone: (201) 441-4224
Published six times a year
www.balloonsandparties.com

Country Business

707 Kautz Road
St. Charles, Illinois
Phone: (386) 447-6304
Published seven times a year
www.sampler.com

DMNews

P.O. Box 20-37
Skokie, IL 60078-7937
Phone: (847)588-0675/0676
Published weekly
www.dmnews.com

Flowers

11444 W. Olympic Blvd.
Los Angeles, CA 90064
Phone: 1-800-321-2654
Published monthly by Teleflora
www.myTeleflora.com

Gift Basket Review

Published by Festivities Publications
815 Haines St.
Jacksonville, FL 32206-6025
Phone: 1-800-SAY-MEET
www.festivities-pub.com

Gifts and Tablewares

1450 Don Mills Road
Don Mills Ontario
M3B 2X7 Canada
Phone: 1-800-387-0273 (Press 1, Dial 2068)
Fax: (416) 442-2213
www.gifts-and-tablewares.com

Gifts and Decorative Accessories

360 Park Avenue South
New York, NY 10010
Phone: (646) 746-6400
Fax: (646) 746-7431
www.giftsanddec.com

The Gifts and Decorative Accessories Buyer's Directory

360 Park Avenue South
New York, NY 10010
Phone: (646) 746-6400
Fax: (646) 746-7431
(Received free with subscription to
Gifts and Decorative Accessories Magazine.)
www.giftsanddec.com

Giftware Business

2950 E. 31st Street, Suite 100
Santa Monica, CA 90405-3037
Phone: (310) 396-6006
Published monthly
www.giftwarebusiness.com

Giftware News

Talcott Communications
20 North Wacker Drive, Suite 1865
Chicago, IL 60606
Phone: (312) 849-2220
Published monthly
www.giftwarenews.com

Greetings Etc.

Published by Edgell Communications
4 Middlebury Boulevard
Randolph, NJ 07869-1111
Published six times per year
Phone: (973) 252-0100
Fax: (973) 252-9020
www.greetingsmagazine.com

Museum Store

Museum Store Association
4100 E. Mississippi Ave., Suite 800
Denver, CO 80246
Phone: (303) 504-9223
Published quarterly
www.museumdistrict.com

Souvenirs, Gifts and Novelties

7000 Terminal Square, Suite 210
Upper Darby, PA 19082
Phone: (610) 734-2420
Published eight times a year
www.souvnovmag.com

SELECTED NATIONAL BUSINESS ASSOCIATIONS

AMERICAN ASSOCIATION OF AFRICAN-AMERICAN WOMEN BUSINESS OWNERS
3363 Alden Place, NE,
Washington, DC 20019
Phone and Fax: (202) 399-3645
www.blackpgs.com/aawboa.

AMERICAN BUSINESS WOMEN'S ASSOCIATION (ABWA)
P. O. Box 8728
9100 Ward Parkway
Kansas City. MO 64114-0728
Phone: 1-800-228-0007
Fax: (816) 361-4991
www.ABWA.org

NATIONAL ASSOCIATION FOR THE SELF EMPLOYED (NASE)
P.O.B. 612067
DFW Airport
Dallas, TX 75261-2067
Phone: 1-800-232-6273
www.NASE.org

NATIONAL ASSOCIATION OF WOMEN BUSINESS OWNERS (NAWBO)
1100 Wayne Avenue STE. 830
Silver Spring, MD 20910
Phone: 1-800-55-NAWBO
Fax: (703) 506-3266
www.NAWBO.org

BOOKS

Adams, Rob (2002). <u>A Good Kick in the Ass</u>. New York: Crown Business.

Alarid, William and Berle, Gustav (1997). <u>Free Help From Uncle Sam to Start Your Own Business (Or Expand the One You Have), 4th ed</u>. Santa Maria, CA: Puma Pub. Company.

Applegate, Jane (1998). <u>201 Great Ideas For Your Small Business</u>. New York: Bloomberg Press.

Bean, Roger and Radford, Russell (2000). <u>Powerful Products: Strategic Management of Successful New Product Development</u>. New York: AMACOM

Berry, Tim (1998). <u>Hurdle: The Book on Business</u>. Eugene, OR: Palo Alto Software, Inc.

Birkeland, Peter M (2002). <u>Franchising Dreams: the Lure of Entrepreneurship in America</u>. Chicago: University of Chicago Press.

Birkinshaw, Julian (2000). <u>Entrepreneurship in the Global Firm</u>. Thousand Oaks, CA: SAGE Publication.

Birley, Sue (1998). <u>Entrepreneurship</u>. Brookfield, VT: Ashgate.

Boston, Thomas D. and Century Foundation (1999). <u>Affirmative Action and Black Entrepreneurship</u>. New York: Routledge.

Butler, John (2001). <u>E-Commerce and Entrepreneurship</u>. Greenwich, CT: Information Age Publishers.

Burgess, Stephen (2002). <u>Managing Information Technology in Small Business: Challenges and Solutions</u>. Hershey, PA: Idea Group Publication.

Canefield, Jack, Hansen, Mark Victor, and Hewitt, Les (2000). <u>The Power of Focus: How to Hit Your Business, Personal and Financial Targets with Absolute Certainty</u>. Deerfield Beach, FL: Health Communications, Inc.

Carey, Charles W. (2002). <u>American Inventors, Entrepreneurs, and Business Visionaries</u>. New York: Facts on File.

Cartwright, Roger and NetLibrary, Inc. (2002). <u>The Entrepreneurial Individual</u>. Oxford, UK: Capstone Pub.

Cheney, Karen and Alderman, Lesley (1997). <u>How to Start a Successful Home Business</u>. New York: Warner Books.

Cleaver, Joanne Y. (1999). <u>Find & Keep Customers for Your Small Business</u>. Chicago: CCH Incorp.

Coulter, Mary (2001). <u>Entrepreneurship in Action</u>. Upper Saddle River, NJ: Prentice Hall.

Crainer, Stuart (2000). <u>Generation Entrepreneur: Shape Today's Business Reality, Create Tomorrow's Wealth, Do Your Own Thing</u>. London: Financial Times Prentice Hall.

Da Costa, Eduardo (2001). <u>Global E-Commerce Strategies for Small Business</u>. Cambridge, MA: MIT Press.

Debelak, Don (2001). <u>Think Big: Nine Ways to Make Millions from Your Ideas</u>. Irvine, CA: Entrepreneur Press.

Dees, J. Gregory, Emerson, Jed and Economy, Peter (2002). <u>Strategic Tools for Social Entrepreneurs: Enhancing the Performance of Your Enterprising Nonprofit</u>. Somerset, NJ: John Wiley and Sons, Inc.

DeLuca, Fred and Hayes, John Phillip (2000). <u>Start Small, Finish Big: Fifteen Key Lessons To Start –and Run—Your Own Successful Business</u>. New York: Warner Books.

Fick, David S. (2002). <u>Entrepreneurship in Africa, A Study of Success</u>. Westport, CT: Quorum Books.

Foley, James F (1999). <u>The Global Entrepreneur: Taking Your Business International</u>. Chicago: Dearborn.

Gerber, Michael E. (1995). <u>The E-Myth Revisited: Why Most Small Business Don't Work and What to Do About It</u>. New York: Harper Collins Publishers.

Goltz, Jay with Oesterricher, Judy (1998). <u>The Street-Smart Entrepreneur: 133 Tough Lessons I Learned the Hard Way</u>. Omaha, NB: Addicus Books.

Gravely, Melvin J (1995). <u>The Black Entrepreneur's Guide to Success</u>. Edgewood, MD: Duncan & Duncan.

Gravely, Melvin J., II (1997). <u>Making It Your Business: The Personal Transition from Employee to Entrepreneur</u>. Cincinnati: Impact Group Consultants.

Hall, Doug (2001). Jump Start Your Business Brain. Cincinnati: Brain Brew Books.

Hayes, Cassandra (2002). Black Enterprise Guide to Building Your Career. New York: John Wiley.

Hisrich, Robert D and Peters, Michael P. (1995). Entrepreneurship: Starting, Developing, and Managing A New Enterprise 3rd ed. Chicago: Irwin.

Hitt, Michael A. (2002). Strategic Entrepreneurship: Creating A New Integrated Mindset. Malden, MA: Blackwell.

Inman, Katherine (2000). Women's Resources in Business Start-up: A Study of Black and White Women Entrepreneurs. New York: Garland Publisher.

Janal, Daniel S. (1997). 101 Successful Businesses You Can Start on the Internet. New York: Van Nostrand Reinhold.

Johnson, Van R. (2000). Entrepreneurial Management and Public Policy. Huntington, NY: Nova Science Publishers.

Kijakazi, Kilolo (1997). African-American Economic Development and Small Business Ownership. New York: Garland Pub.

Kotter, John P. and Cohen, Dan S. (2002). The Heart of Change: Real-Life Stories of How People Change Their Organizations. Watertown, MA: Harvard Business School Press.

Krass, Peter (1999). The Book of Entrepreneur's Wisdom, Classic Writings by Legendary Entrepreneurs. Somerset, NJ: John Wiley & Sons.

Kuratko, Donald F. and Hodgetts, Richard M. (2000). Entrepreneurship: A Contemporary Approach. Fort Worth, TX: Dryden Press.

Lacy, Harold R. (1998). Financing Your Business Dreams with Other People's Money: How and Where to Find Money for Start-up and Growing Businesses. Traverse City, MI: Sage Creek Press.

Lane, Marc J. (2001). Advising Entrepreneurs: Dynamic Strategies For Financial Growth. New York: Wiley.

Lipman, Frederick D. (1998). Financing Your Business with Venture Capital: Strategies to Grow Your Enterprise with Outside Investors. Rocklin, CA: Prima.

Lodish, Leonard, Morgan, Howard Lee, and Kallianpur, Amy (2001). Entrepreneurial Marketing: Lessons from Wharton's Pioneering MBA Course. New York: Wiley.

McDaniel, Bruce (2002). Entrepreneurship and Innovation: An Economic Approach. Armonk, NY: M.E. Sharpe.

Meyers, G. Dale and Heppard, Kurt A. (2000). Entrepreneurship As Strategy: Competing on the Entrepreneurial Edge. Thousand Oaks, CA: SAGE Publications, Inc.

Moore, Dorothy P. and Buttner, E. Holly (1997). Women Entrepreneurs: Moving Beyond The Glass Ceiling. Thousand Oaks, CA: SAGE Publications.

Murtha, Thomas P., Lenway, Stephanie Ann, and Hart, Jeffrey A. (2003). Managing New Industry Creation: Global Knowledge Formation and Entrepreneurship in High Technology. Palo Alto, CA: Stanford University Press.

Oden, Howard W. (1997). Managing Corporate Culture, Innovation, and Entrepreneurship. Westport, CT.: Quorum Books.

Ryan, Rob (2001). Smartups. New York: Cornell University Press.

Sexton, Donald L (1999). The Blackwell Handbook of Entrepreneurship. Malden, MA: Blackwell Business.

Sharma, Poonam (1999). The Harvard Entrepreneur's Club Guide to Starting Your Own Business. New York: John Wiley.

Stephenson, James (2001). Entrepreneur's Ultimate Start-up Directory. Irvine, CA: Entrepreneur Press.

Stolze, William (1996). Start Up: An Entrepreneur's Guide to Launching and Managing a New Business. Hawthorne, NJ: Career Press.

Sullivan, Robert (1998). The Small Business Start-Up Guide. Great Falls, VA: Information International.

Sullivan, William R. (1997). Entrepreneur Magazine: Human Resources for Small Business. New York: John Wiley.

Sutton, Garrett et al (2001). Own Your Own Corporation: Why the Rich Own Their Own Companies and Everyone Else Works For Them. New York: Warner Books.

Tabrrok, Alexander (2002). Entrepreneurial Economics: Bright Ideas from the Dismal Science. New York: Oxford University Press.

Turner, Colin (2002). Lead to Succeed: Creating Entrepreneurial Organizations. New York, London: Texere.

Wallace, Robert L (2000). Soul Food: 52 Principles of Black Entrepreneurial Success. Cambridge, MA: Perseus Pub.

Williams, Bernadette (2002). Black Enterprise Guide to Technology for Entrepreneurs. New York: Wiley.

Williams, Edward E. and Thompson, James R. (1998). Entrepreneurship and Productivity. Lanham, MD: University Press of America.

Woodard, Michael D (1997). Black Entrepreneurs in America: Stories of Struggle and Success. New Brunswick, NJ: Rutgers University Press.

Young, Ruth C, Francis, Joe D, and Young, Christopher H. (1999). Entrepreneurship, Private and Public. Lanham, MD: University Press of America.

INDEXES

Business Periodicals Index. New York: Wilson.
Subject index to articles in the fields of accounting, advertising, public relations, banking, economics, finance and investments, insurance, labor, management, marketing, and taxation. Also includes information on specific businesses, industries, and trades.

Readers' Guide to Periodical Literature. New York: Wilson.
Author and subject index to the contents of over 150 general and nontechnical magazines. A good starting point for finding information on a wide variety of topics.

Social Sciences and Humanities Index. Vols. 1-27, 1916-1974, formerly called International Index. Author and subject index to periodicals in the fields of anthropology, economics, environmental science, geography, law and criminology, political science, psychology public administration, and sociology.

DICTIONARIES AND ENCYCLOPEDIAS

Middle Market Directory. New York: Dun and Bradstreet. Annual. This directory provides information about companies whose net worth ranges from $500,000 to $900,000, including utilities, transportation companies, banks and trust companies, stockbrokers, mutual and stock insurance companies, wholesalers, and retailers. The companies are listed alphabetically, geographically, and by product classification (S.I.C., Standard Industrial Classification).

Million Dollar Directory. New York: Dun and Bradstreet. Annual. Arranged as is Middle Market Directory. This compilation provides information about companies with a net worth of $1 million or more. It also contains a management directory that lists officers and directors and their affiliations.

Poor's Register of Corporations, Directors and Executives, United States and Canada.
New York: Standard and Poor's Corporation. Annual. Volume I contains alphabetical listing of corporations with directors and executives. Volume 2 is a register of directors and executives of the companies listed in Volume 1. Volume 3 contains Standard Industrial Classification and geographical indexes. Supplements are issued in April, July, and October.

List of Small Business Investment Companies. Washington: U.S. Government Printing Office. Irregular.

National Minority Business Directory. Minneapolis: National Minority Business Directories. Annual. This specialized directory lists over 7,000 minority firms (50 percent or more owned by minority group members), classified by product. A cross-reference index aids in finding the appropriate classification. Computer disks are also available. Published by TRY US Resources, Inc. (612) 781-6819.

Thomas Register of American Manufacturers. New York: Thomas Publishing Company. Annual. Manufacturers are arranged according to product, and the manufacturers of each product are listed geographically. Alphabetical indexes to manufacturers, trade names, and specific products facilitate its use.

SPECIAL LISTS

Black Enterprise. New York, Monthly. The "top-100" black-owned businesses that gross more than $1 million annually are listed in the June issue each year.

Forbes. New York. Semi-monthly. The "Annual Report on American Industry" is in the first issue each year. It lists companies according to profitability, growth and pure stock gain over a five-year period. The "Annual Directory Issue" (May 15) ranks the top 500 corporations in sales, stock market value, assets, and profits.

Fortune. New York. Semi-monthly. "The Directory of Largest Corporations" is an annual feature in several parts. The May issue lists the 500 largest U.S. industrial companies by sales. The June issue lists the second-largest 500 U.S. industrial companies. The July issue lists the largest nonindustrial corporations and the fifty largest companies in banking, life insurance, diversified financial services, retailing, transportation, and utilities. The August issue lists the largest corporations outside the United States, and the September issue lists the 300 largest corporations outside the United States, and the September issue lists the 300 largest banks outside the country.

Encyclopedia of Associations. Detroit: Gale Research. Revised approximately every two years. This classified directory lists over 12,000 organized groups. It lists for each, the address, phone number, chief official, a description, publications, and other pertinent information. The alphabetical and key-word index is helpful in locating an association if one does not know its exact name. Supplementary lists of new associations are issued quarterly.

The Foundation Directory. New York: Compiled by the Foundation Center and distributed by Columbia University Press, This directory lists foundations by state. Each entry includes the corporate names, address, purpose, activities, and pertinent financial data.

ATLASES AND MAPS

Ginsburg, Norton. Atlas of Economic Development. Chicago: University of Chicago Press. This atlas offers graphic representations of data on population, land resources, transportation, energy generation and consumption. Each map is accompanied by textual material explaining and summarizing the analyzed data.

Rand McNally Commercial Atlas and Marketing Guide. New York: Rand McNally, Annual. Limited to U.S. marketing data, this atlas provides summaries and analyses of statistics by state in the areas of agriculture, manufacturing, population, retail trade, and transportation.

BIBLIOGRAPHIES AND GUIDES

Coman, Edwin T. Sources of Business Information. rev. ed. Berkeley and Los Angeles: University of California Press. . The first four chapters of this guide deal with methodology and the range of business sources. The remaining chapters treat such specific fields as accounting, real estate and insurance, and management. Limited to American and Canadian sources, and a few from England.

Encyclopedia of Business Information Sources. 2 vols. Detroit: Gale. Volume I is organized alphabetically by topic, with sub headings by type of source. Lists primary and secondary sources of information.

PERIODICALS

Academy of Management Journal. Tampa, FL., Quarterly.

Accounting Review. Sarasota, Fl.: American Accounting Association. Quarterly.

Administrative Science Quarterly. Ithaca, NY: Cornell University Graduate School of Business and Public Administration. Quarterly.

Black Enterprise. New York. Monthly.

Business Week. New York: McGraw-Hill. Weekly.

Commerce America. Washington: U.S. Department of Commerce. Bi-weekly. Order from U.S. Government Printing Office.

Dun's Review. New York: Dun & Bradstreet. Monthly.

Federal Reserve Bulletin. Washington: U.S. Board of Governors of the Federal Reserve System. Monthly.

Forbes. New York. Semimonthly.

Fortune. New York, Semimonthly.

Harvard Business Review. Boston: Harvard University Graduate School of Business Administration. Monthly.

Industry Week. Cleveland, OH: Penton Publishing Company. Weekly.

Money. Chicago. Monthly.

Monthly Labor Review. Washington: U.S. Government Printing Office. Monthly

Nation's Business. Washington: Chamber of Commerce of the United States. Monthly.

Survey of Current Business. Washington: U.S. Department of Commerce. Order from U.S. Government Printing Office. Monthly. Supplemented weekly by Business Statistics.

Wall Street Journal. New York: Dow Jones. 5 issues per week.

ADDITIONAL GENERAL REFERENCES

http://www.census.gov/epcd/mwb97/us/us.html#Black - Census Bureau information for minority and women-owned businesses

http://www.census.gov/prod/ec97/e97cs-2.pdf - census information

http://www.census.gov/Press-Release/www/2001/cb01-61.html - women-owned businesses, numbers from 1997

http://www.nfwbo.org/minority/AllMinority.pdf - minority women business owners data

ANNUAL STATEMENT STUDIES	The Risk Management Association (Formerly Robert Morris Associates) One Liberty Place 1650 Market Street, Suite 2300 Philadelphia, PA 19103 Phone: 1-800-677-7621; (215) 446-4000 Fax: (215) 446-4101 www.rmahq.org
KEY BUSINESS RATIOS	The D&B Corporation 103 JFK Parkway Short Hills, NJ 07078 Phone:1- 800-234-3867 For International Inquiries – 1-800-932-0025 www.dnb.com

Appendix

SAMPLE BUSINESS FORMS

"For all the trials and tears of time, for every hill I

have to climb, my heart sings but a grateful song--

these are the things that make me strong."

Anonymous

SAMPLE PURCHASE ORDER FORM

PURCHASE ORDER

Date:_____   P.O. # _____
                                                (assign in sequence)

TO: (NAME OF SUPPLIER)

How to Ship: (UPS or other)
Terms: (will pay when billed, etc.)

Deliver By: (date needed)

BILL TO: (NAME AND ADDRESS OF FIRM TO RECEIVE BILL)

Shipping & Packing Instructions:

SHIP TO: (NAME AND ADDRESS OF WHERE GOODS SHOULD BE SENT)

Quantity	Item #	Description	Unit Cost	Discount	Total

_____
GRAND TOTAL

Ordered by:_____

NOTE Please show our order # on all shipments or correspondence, and advise if unable to meet required delivery date.

ANY CHANGES IN THIS PURCHASE ORDER MUST BE IN WRITING

Any such failure that results in documentable third party costs will be deducted from the vendor's invoice. Failure on the part of vendor to meet terms and delivery dates will void this Purchase Order unless such charges are authorized in revised Purchase Order.

BILLING STATEMENT

FIRM NAME, ADDRESS AND CONTACT NUMBERS

Statement Date:_____   **Acct. No.:**_____

(Please refer to this number in all your correspondence)

TO: CUSTOMER NAME

Date	Terms	Items or Services Purchased	Amount	Remarks

Please Pay This Amount: _____

Current	30 days	60 days	90 days and over

*Note: Terms Net _____ Days

PETTY CASH RECORD

DATE	PAID TO	FOR	APPROVED BY	BALANCE ON HAND

BALANCE SHEET

ASSETS

	Present Year	Prior Year

Current Assets
   Cash (in hand, in banks)
    Accounts receivable (subtract
     allowance for bad debts)
   Inventories
   Prepayments
   Investments (at cost)
   Other _____

Total current assets:

Fixed Assets
   Land
   Buildings
   Refrigeration Units
   Office Equipment
   Other _____
    Subtotal
   Less accumulated depreciation
Net fixed assets:
Other assets and deferred charges
Intangibles (goodwill, patents, trademarks)

Total assets

LIABILITIES

Current Liabilities:
   Accounts payable
   Notes payable
   Accrued expenses payable
   Federal and state income taxes payable
   Other _____
Total current liabilities

Long Term Liabilities
   Interest (notes payable after one year)
   Other _____
Total liabilities:

INCOME STATEMENT

	Present Year	Prior Year
Revenues:		
Net Sales (operating revenues, less discounts)	_____	_____
Other income:	_____	_____
Total revenue:	_____	_____
Cost of Sales:		
Inventory	_____	_____
Royalties	_____	_____
Other _____	_____	_____
Total cost of sales:	_____	_____
Gross profit or loss:	_____	_____
Operating Expenses		
Selling Expense (Adv., payroll, travel, entertainment, etc.)	_____	_____
General Administration (Heat, light, rent, etc.)	_____	_____
Other _____	_____	_____
Net income before taxes:	_____	_____
Income taxes:	_____	_____
Net Profit:	_____	_____

"There is no success unless you have successors."

M.G.L.J.

NOTES

[1] http://www.womensbusinessresearch.org/Research/5-6-2003/5-6-2003.html

[2] http://www.aboutflowers.com/press_b1.html#

[3] American Floral Endowment, "Understanding Floral Product Buying Patterns when purchasing Birthday Gifts." by Doreen Zavada for Ipsos-NPD, Inc., April 2002 . Web site: www.endowment.org/specialreports/marketing.htm

[4] American Floral Endowment, "Buying Floral Products on the Internet" by Doreen Zavada for Ipsos-NPD, Inc., April 2002 . Web site: www.endowment.org/specialreports/marketing.html

[5] Ibid

[6] Kenneth Lawyer and Clifford Baumback, How to Organize and Operate a Small Business, 6th Edition (Upper Saddle River, NJ: Prentice Hall, 1979, p. 56.

[7] Hal B. Pickel, "Personality and Success: An Evaluation of Personal Characteristics of Successful Small Business Managers," Small Business Research Series No. 4. Small Business Administration (Washington, DC: G.P.O.), 1964.

[8] Small Business Administration, "Keys to Business Success," Office of Management Assistance (1973), p. 37.

[9] James F. DeCarlo and Paul Lyons, " A Comparison of Selected Personal Characteristics of Minority and Non-Minority Female Entrepreneurs," Journal of Small Business Management, 17 October 1979, pp.25-26.

[10] Ibid, p. 25

[11] Ibid

[12] William Glueck, "Entrepreneurial and Family Firms," Management (Hinsdale, Illinois: Dryden Press, 1977), p. 57.

[13] Ibid, p. 50

[14] Ralph Stogdill, Handbook of Leadership (New York: The Free Press, 1974), pp. 76-82.

[15] Ibid, p. 167

[16] Charles B. Swayne and William R. Tucker, <u>The Effective Entrepreneur</u> (Morristown, NJ: General Learning Press, 1973), p. 35.

[17] I*bid., p. 35*

[18] Keith Davis, <u>Human Behavior at Work</u> (New York: McGraw Hill, Inc., 1977) p. 26.

[19] Kenneth R. Van Voorhis, <u>Entrepreneurship and Small Business Management</u> (Boston: Allyn & Bacon, 1980), p. 29.

"You will pass those who discouraged you from pursuing

your entrepreneurial dreams on the stairway to success.

They will be sitting on the steps, still passing out negative

thoughts and going nowhere"

M.G.L.J.

A BUSINESS OF YOUR OWN
Business Publications and Services for the Entrepreneurial Woman

"Our purpose is to assist the entrepreneurial woman in pulling together the intricate components necessary to make a small business a success!!!"

FACT SHEET

A BUSINESS OF YOUR OWN is a multifaceted service firm that specializes in business publications and services designed to assist women in starting and managing small businesses.

A BUSINESS OF YOUR OWN publishes information that inspire, motivate, educate and help the female entrepreneur grow and develop skills to manage a successful business. Our publications range from basic startup manuals to detailed guide books for implementing and managing a specific business.

A BUSINESS OF YOUR OWN does more than just present the nuts and bolts of initiating a business between the covers of a manual. We are different because entrepreneurial women are different! We also offer strategy sessions, workshops, seminars, business development retreats, and much more...

ABOUT OUR COMPREHENSIVE START UP MANUALS.......

The informational publications from A BUSINESS OF YOUR OWN reflect an enormous amount of in-depth research and the expertise of many noted professionals. Our comprehensive business start-up publications utilize a uniquely designed step-by-step, hands-on approach to business formulation. Crucial business development and management information is provided in an easy to understand format followed by questions for the entrepreneur to address. The summarization of the answers to these questions will enable the entrepreneurially minded woman in pulling together the major components of their business. Worksheets are provided for the purpose of providing assistance in preparing a business plan. All business start-up publications are designed so that upon completion, the entrepreneur will have a detailed business plan for their venture.

**Our manuals are: *Currently researched   *Informational *Practical *Systematic *Motivational
*Comprehensive *Easy to understand *Designed for the Entrepreneurial Woman**

Additional Publications for the Entrepreneurial Woman

- "So You're Thinking About Starting a Business" A Comprehensive General Start Up Manual" $49.95
- Starting a Secretarial Service $59.95
- Starting an Antique Business $59.95
- Starting a Public Relations Firm $59.95
- Starting a Child Care Center $49.95 (Paperback-81/2 by 11)
- Starting a Clothing Boutique $59.95
- Starting a Business to Sell Your Craft Items $59.95
- Starting a Franchise $59.95
- Starting a Mail Order Business $59.95
- Starting a Home Based Business $59.95
- Starting a Business to Sell Your Art Work $59.95

Shipping and Handling Costs: $4.00/manual ▲ *Traditional Discounts Offered to the Trade.*

A BUSINESS OF YOUR OWN
P.O.B. 210662 ■ Nashville, Tennessee 37221-0662
Phone: (615) 646-3708 ■ Fax: (615) 662-8584
E-mail: Success@womaninbiz.com   Website: www.ABusinessofYourOwn.com

Notes

CIC Craglist.edu

LaVergne, TN USA
30 November 2009

165481LV00001B/20/A